HIK

THE ULTIMATE NATURAL PRESCRIPTION

FOR HEALTH AND WELLNESS

BY PHILIP FERRANTI

AND CECILIA LEVYA

WITH JOIE GOODKIN

D0483341

 KENDALL/HUNT PUBLISHING COMPANY
4050 Westmark Drive   Dubuque, Iowa 52002

This Kendall/Hunt book is available at special quantity discounts for bulk purchases for sales promotions, premiums, fund-raising, and educational needs. For details call

Kendall/Hunt Publishing Company
4050 Westmark Drive
P.O. Box 1840
Dubuque, IA 52004-1840
Phone: 1-800-228-0810
Fax: 1-800-772-9165
www.kendallhunt.com

Copy Editor: Kris Fulsaas

Creative Director: Joie Goodkin

Cover and interior design, illustration: Lightbourne Images, copyright © 1997

Cover photo: Indian Peaks Wilderness, Glenn Randall, courtesy of The Hill Gallery, Aspen, Colorado

Copyright © 1997 by Philip Ferranti

ISBN: 0-7872-3497-4

Library of Congress Catalog Number: 97-70403

Printed in the United States of America

10   9   8   7   6   5   4   3   2   1

OTHER BOOKS BY PHILIP FERRANTI

75 GREAT HIKES IN AND NEAR PALM SPRINGS AND THE COACHELLA VALLEY

Discover Southern California's inland mountain and desert empire with this first ever book on the over 750 miles of hiking trails in and near the desert resort cities of Palm Springs and Palm Desert—an area containing some of the finest winter/spring hikes anywhere in the United States. Beautiful and exotic trails are accented by the fantastic pristine natural setiings highlighted in this guide including: Joshua Tree National Park, The Palm Springs Indian Canyons, the Mecca Wilderness Area, the Santa Rosa and San Jacinto Mountains, the top of the Tram and Idyllwild and the famed Pacific Crest Trail.

Endless sunny and warm days complements this beautiful area with some of the best winter/spring weather found in the United States—perfect for a hiking vacation or a weekend get-away! This guide book offers a user friendly format of maps, photos, hiking length/time/elevation gain/difficulty and the best time of year to enjoy each trail.

Order From: Kendall/Hunt Publishing Company
                  1-800-228-0810 Fax: 1-800-772-9165

For Information on the Coachella Valley call:
The Palm Desert Chamber of Commerce 800-873-2428
Fax: 619-346-3263

COLORADO STATE PARKS: A COMPLETE RECREATION GUIDE

Now available for the first time, *Colorado State Parks* represents the most comprehensive recreational guide to all of Colorado's breathtaking 40 state parks, and highlights the complete recreational activities found during each of Colorado's diverse four seasons. Hikers, boaters, campers, picnickers, bikers, fishermen, equestrians, and other outdoor enthusiasts will find a wealth of valuable information in this guide, including maps, photos, park hours, fees, campsite availability, and safety tips. The appendix for this book contains one of the most concentrated collections of phone numbers and addresses for every agency, group, club or organization found in the state specializing in outdoor activities. This guide is a must read for anyone who enjoys all the fabled beauty and recreational opportunities Colorado offers. Order from: The Mountaineers Books, 1-800-553-4453/Fax 206-223-6306, 24 hours a day.

CONTENTS

FOREWORD

When I was a little girl, my favorite activities involved nature. I could crouch over a daisy for what seemed like hours, pluck at its petals and marvel at its construction.

When I grew older, I replaced the "n" in nature with an "m" and became "mature." I wore lipstick, bought gold hoop earrings, gabbed on the telephone for hours and cruised around town indefinitely in a convertible.

What happened to nature? Too busy . . . gotta get into college, get married, get a job, run a business, raise my child, be part of a family. . . .

When I really got "older," I retired and discovered rapture. I went hiking. Wow! I loved the way hiking made me feel. It touched and filled all my senses. I loved the feel of the earth beneath my feet, the smell of the air, the touch of the rocks—the "record keepers" as my Native American friends call them. Most of all, I loved the enveloping sense of the stillness when I was enfolded by nature, awed by its serenity.

It wasn't until I had hiked for several years that I thought back to those rare times in my life when I took the time to walk in the woods. I remember once lugging home an odd-shaped piece of dead tree trunk because there was something about it "that would be perfect for the coffee table."

In those days hiking would have conjured images of red-and black-checkered flannel shirts, pickup trucks, and geezers trudging around in forests. I missed a lot by having little awareness of the outdoors. It was to be many years before I realized that being in nature was the complement and completion needed to experience life to its fullest.

It was an indescribable joy to reach a mountain peak, and then relax and munch lunch with hiking buddies, sharing food and our great love of the majesty and beauty of nature. The elevation gain was, literally, for me a climb to God. To sit on a rock and contemplate, meditate, read, or just inhale deeply out there is one of the greatest gifts and joys I have known.

On the trail, hiking with organized outdoor club people and making new friends, it is thrilling to share the experience of just being yourself. Hikers care about what you are saying, not what you are wearing. Hikers are just plain folks. Anyone can hike. There is no competition, nothing to judge and nothing to sell. The camaraderie and laughter, the friendships that develop, the catharsis of telling close friends about things in your life that surprise you by coming to mind on the trail—all are part of the gestalt of the experience.

You're just out there and you can't help but love it! You're just another one of God's natural creatures and there is no judgment, just joy! I hope this book reaches many other people like me.

Joie Goodkin

PREFACE

America is a land and culture that have always been marked by people pushing back new frontiers, not only geographically but socially and technologically as well. In this century especially, psychologists and others have offered an endless stream of strategies for feeling better, becoming successful, discovering ourselves, and realizing the "American Dream." Perhaps if nothing else, this trend has supported the notion that wellness and health are a composite of many complementary regimens and decisions, that no one activity can respond to the multiple needs and aspects of any human being. The challenge then is to find and apply those activities that do most to enhance our total well-being.

I believe that we are about to see great changes in our society. One of the most important will be people's turning away from media-entertainment-technology, an all-too-passive distraction, to those activities that offer a direct, honest, in-touch participation—involvements that facilitate real wellness rather than hyped promises. We will begin demanding positive payoffs that "do something."

Imagine someone advising you at sixteen to invest just $100 in a stock that would grow at such a rate that when you are fifty years old you would be a multimillionaire. Your financial security would be assured for life. This kind of opportunity is extremely rare. But suppose that during your youth, someone introduced you to an outdoor activity that, if faithfully practiced and enjoyed, would reap lifelong benefits of an astounding magnitude—benefits that would almost guarantee enhanced, lifelong, high-quality health and wellness.

This book is about such an activity: hiking. And this activity is not a rare, few-can-do-this pursuit. Almost anyone physically capable of walking can hike. But, as with everything else in life, people need to "choose it and do it" if they are to gain the benefits that come from this healthiest of outdoor pursuits.

This book is more devoted to the "why" of hiking than the "how." This book shares how hiking affects "wellness." Individual chapters offer testimony from the lives of people who hike as a regular part of their daily lifestyle.

There are many books written about backpacking, an extended hike into the wilderness where the hiker stays out at least overnight and carries all their food, equipment, and sleeping gear. This book, however, focuses on dayhiking, walking through nature but not staying overnight.

Why write such a book on such a simple activity as hiking? Because hiking, in its simplicity, actually meets real human needs, consistently, honestly, and effectively. There are too many promised cures for all that ails us; too many hyped, expensive, sometimes even harmful remedies, practices, and quick fixes that don't work or work so poorly as to not merit our using them. However, hiking is an inexpensive pastime that benefits the participant far more than anyone else.

Hiking brings you into the natural world. No passive video or television images here. Hiking involves walking through nature, climbing hills, stretching, examining rocks, flowers, trees, and waterways with nose, eyes, ears, and hands. Hiking demands that you get *into* the scenes you walk through, experience them directly by sweat, preparation, and discipline. Hiking is a "doing" thing.

More than 155 million adult Americans have yet to discover the universal and enjoyable benefits of hiking. This book is written especially for you, in the hopes of inspiring you to take up hiking, share this pleasurable pastime with your children and friends, and thereby gain the advantages that almost 45 million Americans have already discovered.

Those who are already hikers will find this book a great affirmation of the healthy lifestyle they have chosen, offering them perhaps even additional insights into why they so much like and benefit from their adventures on the trail.

Whether you are a veteran dayhiker or are brand-new to this activity—welcome to the ultimate natural prescription for health and wellness: hiking!

Philip Ferranti

ACKNOWLEDGMENTS

Excerpt from *John Muir Apostle of Nature* by Thurman Wilkins. Copyright © 1995. By permission of the University of Oklahoma Press, Norman.

Excerpt from *Saanichtoni* 1974, "My Heart Soars" by Chief Dan George. By permission of Hancock House Publishers, Baine, WA

Excerpt from *The Way to Rainy Mountain* by N. Scott Momaday 1969. By permission of the University of New Mexico Press, Albuquerque.

Excerpt from the *Arizona Republic*. By permission.

Excerpt from *The Wilderness World of John Muir*, edited by Edwin Way Teale. Copyright © 1954 by Edwin Way Teale. Copyright © renewed 1982 by Nellie D. Teale. Reprinted by permission of Houghton Mifflin Co. All rights reserved.

From *Markings* by Dag Hammarskjold, trans., Auden/Sjoberg. Translation copyright © 1964 by Alfred A. Knopf, Inc. and Faber & Faber Ltd. Reprinted by permission of Alfred A. Knopf, Inc.

"Desert Melody" by Alice Brooke McReynolds, with grateful permission.

Excerpt from *The Celestine Prophecy* by James Redfield. Copyright © 1993. Warner Books, New York.

Introduction
Humankind in Nature

Rediscovering Our
Lost Connection

"In God's wildness lies the hope of the world—the great fresh, unblighted, unredeemed wilderness. The galling harness of civilization drops off, and the wounds heal ere we are aware."

—John Muir, "The Wilderness World of John Muir"

THE MOVE FROM THE LAND TO THE CITY

We once all walked the land—together. Humankind's first "career" was that of a hunter-gatherer. For tens of thousands of years, from our emergence out of our distant past, through the various stone ages and into the ages of metal, people moved about the earth on foot as a normal function of daily living. Walking through nature—hiking—was a necessity. Hunting required fast and steady travel over long distances. The horse was not yet domesticated. Whole tribes and nations migrated on foot to new homelands or pasture lands, summer-to-winter and winter-to-summer. Hunting trails were the first highways; changes of climate drove our ancestors to trek to new feed-

1

ing and hunting grounds out of desperate survival. People experienced an intimate relationship with the land, forests, grasslands, mountains, and rivers.

But our longtime involvement with the land began to change with the advent of the first villages and cities. Farming began replacing the hunt. The city began competing with nature as the source of people's vital connection with life forces and the earth's changing seasons.

Beginning with the first landings of colonists in Virginia and New England, America offered a wild, untamed land, "from sea to shining sea," America the beautiful. Decade after decade, the frontier beckoned to the American spirit to come and enjoy new opportunities and the freedom of open spaces, pure water, and clean air. Whether it was the stunning beauty of Daniel Boone's Kentucky, the spectacular Rocky Mountains of Colorado, or the fertile lands of Oregon and California, every age of American exploration and discovery was followed by the relentless push westward, with the taming of those lands and eventual creation of the rural lifestyle— small villages and towns, farms, and ranches where people lived in dynamic relationship with the seasons and the surrounding countryside.

America was identified as a land where eastern forests pushed against and over Appalachian mountains and into southern swamps, eventually spilling out into the thousand-mile grass-and-prairie lands of the Midwest, which in turn flowed westward, meeting head-on the massive Rocky Mountains. From there, America extended into the deserts of the Great Basin and southwestern mesas and plateaus, before finding relief in the cool Sierra Nevadas and Cascade Mountains of California and Oregon, with the final jewels of American geography being the Columbia and Willamette River valleys, the rain forests, mountains, and waterways of western Washington, and the sun-drenched Mediterranean-like playground of Southern California.

During the nineteenth century, more than 75 percent of Americans lived in rural communities, and the vast majority of people were farmers. Until the early twentieth century, the American Dream included the enriching experiences of our wilderness, our forests, rivers, prairies, mountains, and deserts. For generations, adults fondly remembered their childhood antics along countless riverways, ponds, and lakes, in secluded woods and great, endless sweeps of prairie stretching to infinite horizons— we all had a little of Huck Finn and Tom Sawyer in our youth, experienced a touch of Willa Cather's Midwest or the colorful autumn of New England and its fall colors.

But as with the migration of population in Europe from the villages to the cities, Americans, by the beginning of the twentieth century, began a mass migration to cities and their metropolitan areas. After World War II, the population shift included a surge of people into the suburbs. During the years following the mid-1960s, the dramatic shift of population into urban areas increased. In time, the country witnessed the well-documented decline of the inner cities, the growth in suburban sprawl, and the aggravated assault of pollution on our waterways, open spaces, and clean air. Billboards and advertisement of every kind competed for space along roadways, on buildings, radio, television—wherever we could look, whenever we could hear.

While not restricted by the concentration of massed buildings of the inner city, suburban living is still exposed to most of the cultural, commercial, and media blitz found in city living. In the 1990s, 75 percent of all Americans live in metropolitan areas of over 100,000 population. The shift from rural living to the cities is nearly complete.

The Rat Race

Modern life has drawn humans into cities and surrounding metropolitan environments. The culture of our society, often created in the city, is dispensed through the media, through movies, television programs, magazines, radio, and entertainment. This interaction between city, culture, and people greatly influences all of us, especially children and what they eventually come to believe, want, aspire toward, act upon, and expect. Life for many individuals in our culture is their response or reaction to what culture suggests is "real" and worthy of pursuit.

Technology has been raised to the status of a god in modern society, with conventional wisdom believing that television, the telephone, the computer, radio, the compact disc player, movies, and almost every other product of technology is there to offer the chance for communication, information, and entertainment. Too often, all that this technology really does is offer an effective means for "mass distraction"—endless possibilities for individuals to escape away from themselves, instead of into the sanctuary of themselves.

Young people often base their decision on whether to go to college upon their cultural bias toward what college is supposed to do for them, what they are going to get as a payoff—a job, a better life, more money, prestige. The clothes we wear, the hip phrases we use, how we treat others, our decisions, who our friends are, if and when we marry, if and when we have children, and how we treat those children are all influenced by our interaction with culture. And coloring, flavoring, highlighting all of what we call life is the economic value system of this culture, values that sum up many of our choices: Money is good, what sells has value, what does not sell does not; we are "worth" what we "have" financially and "of worth" if we help someone create a profit. Too often, the pursuit of what the media suggests is worthy of our energies becomes too dominant in of our life—how much we buy for Christmas, for Halloween, Valentines Day, this event and that event.

Geography is a subject in decline. People's experience of nature often becomes what was seen in a movie or on television. Many young people would rather hear a rock concert than a rushing stream. America, in far too many places, no longer celebrates its natural heritage. The world of commerce is drawing us away from realizing the benefits of the natural world—not everywhere but, with 75 percent of us living in metropolitan sprawls, in far too many places.

Americans have coined a phrase that captures all the frustrations of modern life lived in response to the commercial drumbeats of the workplace and the demands of economic survival: the "rat race." Daily, many people rise to face a workday doing jobs that are unfulfilling. We are keenly aware of our public job or career identity. Paid less for doing more, many people look forward to their private lives at home. But especially it is the weekends that Americans covet. The "weekend" has come to mean more than a mere reprieve from the daily routine of work. Like the garages joined to our homes, the weekend offers us the opportunity to tinker with our private lives, build something based more on our desires and interests than the demands and roles of the workplace.

But what happens on those weekends? How many Americans actually build lives that satisfy and free themselves from the pressures and stress that the work week creates? If you would believe the many polls and surveys done during the past ten years concerning quality of life and the burdens of stressful living on today's American, the results show that too many of us fail to show up at work Monday morning refreshed and revitalized.

The simple act of living in cities, surrounded by concrete, steel, asphalt, neon, noise, pollution, and social ills, crowded together, waiting in long lines for gas, groceries, a ticket to our entertainment escapes, etc., all weigh heavy upon our souls and psyches. In cities, there often are no horizons, just skylines. In cities, the stars shine at night, but are difficult to see through the smoke, haze, and light. Something vital to true human living is missing. Nature is in recess.

The Psyche of the City

I've lived in cities; I am no stranger to their ways . . . London, Dublin, San Francisco, San Diego, Vancouver, BC, Denver, Cincinnati. Besides these larger metropolitan areas, I've called home a handful of small towns, with populations less than 100,000. Cities to me are an interesting distraction offering a smorgasbord of culture and ethnic expressions of food, manners, dress, language, and looks. Superimposed upon this melting pot is the corporate/commercial culture of brand names, advertisements, jingles, catch phrases, television personalities, celebrities, and all the other hype of the marketplace that passes itself off as "America" and as life itself. Musical dance numbers sell everything from toilet paper to soft drinks. Neon lights, banners, billboards—all compete to inundate the

6

city dweller with the messages of the consumer-driven culture to buy, buy, buy; look, look, look; spend, spend, spend.

I grew weary staying in the cities. While living in San Francisco I happened upon a Greek immigrant and his family. He invited me over for dinner and shared with me his frustrations of living in the city. "Oh, I can't complain about the money. I earn five times more here than what I made in Athens. But no one seems to be able to slow down long enough to enjoy life, to talk with each other, spend an afternoon discovering who the person you're with really is. So I'm returning to Greece. At least there, people know how to really live."

Cities can do that: offer a narrow vision of what it means to be human. The Greek immigrant and his family's complaints were well founded. Life in the city often pressures the dwellers therein to feel suffocated, driven, hurried, and lacking perspective.

Nature Can Transform Us

As a school boy I remember geography lessons as a celebration of the American landscape. My fellow classmates viewed with awe the natural collage of mountain, prairie, forest, and desert that teachers presented as our rich, American natural heritage. Graduation into adulthood meant more than just job, career, or making my way in the world. It also meant having the freedom to visit and partake of the natural wonders that America represented.

Some of us also remember from our youth experiences such as working on the land, visiting a relative in the country, knowing firsthand the outdoor life of farm or ranch— country living. But life changed, and we often have just memories of times when the land and nature spoke their quiet peace and sang the beautiful melodies of birds; of open fields, sweet with newmown hay and grass, the climb up a hill to survey the kingdom we felt was surely ours for the taking, at least all the way to the nearest creek or swimming hole. The challenge from that youth remains: how to rediscover the wonders of nature, the power of the land.

I have a friend who for years, as a teacher, has introduced high school and college-age young people to the joys of hiking. He tells me that often people who were totally uneasy about being in nature almost instantly were transformed the moment they stepped out on the trail, touched a tree, smelled a flower, and looked to distant horizons. During a hike they expressed their wonder out loud, forging ahead to see what lay over the hill, climbing down into canyon recesses to discover colorful rock formations, challenging themselves with demanding ascents up trails that took them to the heights of mountain overlooks. Instead of stodgy, blank-faced students in the classroom, kids magically transformed into curious, exploratory, challenged youth. Teenage girls who hours before worried about breaking a nail, not being cool, or getting dirty were now besting the boys in the quest for adventure along the trail.

This same teacher invited his students' parents along, and witnessed a similar transformation in them. Once he took a lawyer, who hadn't been outdoors for years, out on a long hike. As they reached the trail's end and began their return, the lawyer quipped, "I don't want to go back; I want to stay out here. I don't care if I ever go back."

While this is an extreme reaction to the joys of hiking and being back in nature, his assertion suggests a phenomenon that I also have witnessed with people I first introduced to hiking: they like the experience in an enthusiastic way that shakes them free from the sedentary mentality they may have lived with for years, and recaptures some vital memories inspired from youthful first encounters with nature. What explains this transformation?

Years ago I was given a dog as a gift. She was my first dog since my teen years, and I spent several weeks just getting her accustomed to me, my home, and her surroundings. During this time, she was somewhat withdrawn, tentative, and quiet. Finally, after securing a good leash, I took her outside for the first time, to walk the nearby golf course. The moment we stepped outside, I witnessed the birth of a "new dog."

Instantly Skitts perked up, a flash of excitement swept over her as her face lightened up, her personality became quite animated, even joyful—she was in her true "element" again, out and about in nature, sniffing grasses, exploring new odors, discovering the world for the first time, it seemed. From that day, I knew that I had a true hiking companion, a real trail dog. And after climbing Colorado peaks over 14,000 feet high with Skitts, hiking hundreds of trails and thousands of miles with her, her enthusiasm has never waned. She is fully alive to her senses in nature, and on the trail. Home again.

I've thought about this experience, and about the transformation that took place with those new hikers I and my friend had taken into the natural world. I juxtapose the blank, empty, lost look of many city folk I've seen with the aliveness of kids, dogs, and adults on the trail, and a theory emerges.

We humans lived in and with nature for tens of thousands of years, following hunting paths, hiking woods, grasslands, and mountain trails. We evolved cosmologies, philosophies, religions, rituals, and traditions based on our interaction with nature. The natural world was our home; hiking was what we did to move about in that world while living out our daily life. Just as my dog Skitts has been imprinted genetically to respond to her place in nature, have not we humans also been impacted down to the very cells and psyches of our so-called "human nature?" Being penned up in cities with their concrete, steel, glass, plastic, pollution; being bombarded by the media, crushed in a flowing sea of people—this is a very recent happening, measured in a few generations versus the almost million years of our primitive, natural heritage.

It feels good to be out in the woods, on a mountain, crossing a desert, looking to distant horizons, thrashing about meadows and grasslands, because that's where our first and true home was. We are meant to relate to nature, smell its intoxicating fragrances, challenge its mountain slopes, feel its solid, reassuring presence beneath our feet, look to far-reaching horizons that open our vision heavenward to the stars and the universe itself. In nature, we become centered in our true selves, grounded in its healing touch, enlivened by the sensual, physical expressions of color, sound, scent, and visual magnificence. The famous naturalist John Muir encouraged people in his day to exit the cities and regain themselves in the wilderness.

The city is artificial and contrived, however necessary it seems. Humans, I believe, are simply at home when hiking a trail. I never fail to feel this warm, inviting familiarity whenever I go into the natural world. Leaving work on Friday afternoon, we regain our freedom "out there." Something heavy and false slips off our shoulders and we are reborn . . . homecoming!

Lifestyles Embracing Rather Than Divorced from Nature

In my more than twenty trips across America, visiting 42 states, I've come to recognize that there are two types of lifestyle in this country. In one, nature is seldom visited, and when it is visited, the event resembles a trip through a fast-food outlet. For example, 2.5 million people visit Zion National Park in a given year, but fewer than 2 percent ever took out backcountry permits or experienced the backcountry trail system. Hit and run. It's true that many people don't go into the backcountry for a variety of reasons such as disability, infirmity due to age, inclement weather, inconvenient illness during one's vacation, etc. But to many people, being outside is alien, strange, unfamiliar, and, under certain circumstances, frightening.

Passive viewing of life, encouraged by television, computers, and the Internet, together with a culture devoted to escapism through entertainment and spectator sports, is a trend that has divorced millions from opportunities of experiencing themselves in a more challenging, vital way. Life is not a collection of sound-bites and images, jingles and one-liners. Those whose lifestyle is divorced from outdoor recreation must somehow add the benefits of hiking through nature. We may have been drawn into the city for economic survival, but we now must reclaim the land in order to regain our real selves. And all over America, people are taking such steps to embrace nature.

The other type of lifestyle is one of close and fond interaction with the land and nature. These people hike, fish, boat, ski, bike, and camp. They know where they live, the physical lay of the land, the roads, rivers, ponds, woods, and high-country trails. They love the land, know it, appreciate it, enjoy it to the full. They can be alone in the wild; they can commune with nature's solitude and feel inspired and comforted throughout the four seasons. Theirs is a love affair with the great outdoors, as necessary to be in as it is to eat. For them, human nature embraces the natural world and it is as integral to their lives as wet is to water. Even when such individuals are working and living in cities, they make time to frequent the outdoors, visiting both city parks and the nearby countryside. Long weekends are often spent miles away, in wilderness or along some beckoning trail.

For years the city folk of Southern California have escaped to the open, sunny desert resorts of the Palm Springs area. More and more of these visitors are searching for something beyond distraction and escape. They are taking to the local trails, both in the deserts and their canyons and in surrounding mountains. Hiking is becoming their lifeline toward finding a true balance in their lives. By hiking the desert-mountain trails that envelop this resort, visitors are releasing the stress, pressures, and overloaded minds they bring with them from city living.

How do I know this? In September 1992 I started a local hiking club. Within three years we had a thousand members enjoying the outdoors, hiking trails both in and out of state. Visitors from all corners of the earth joined us. As a hike leader, I was able to chat with people on my hikes and learn their feelings and observations about what hiking meant to them.

The general feeling was that hiking and being in nature was, for most, a spiritual experience. They felt cleansed, more alive, curious, optimistic, and fun-loving while out in the natural world, during a hike, than where they came from. Hiking was akin to taking a retreat, meditating, getting back to the basics. A feeling of balance returned to their lives. The beauty of nature, peaceful and scenic, touched their hearts and souls. Life seemed more harmonious to them, as they reconnected to their natural heritage. The exercise helped, too!

Hiking is one sure way that people can reconnect with themselves, feel their own bodies as they strain up a challenging mountain slope, experience their own physical and mental energies released and flowing by the exercise hiking affords them, and enjoy the scenic encounters with nature that inspire rejuvenation of heart and soul.

Making Nature More Accessible
In large cities the natural world, though perhaps visible, is often at a distance and has to compete with concrete; people often cannot see the natural world from the city centers. While city parks offer some relief, urban residents need to rethink their priorities for what constitutes a fulfilling lifestyle. Urban planning must come to include natural development and access. Parks, river walkways, and recreational areas must be a part of any city's development plan. What is now successful in cities throughout the United States must be studied and applied in those cities lacking natural access and development.

Colorado is a model state for urban planning that addresses people's need for visiting nature and hiking. In the Grand Valley area that includes the Colorado River, four state parks, and the hub city of Grand Junction, the county and city governments are building a Colorado Riverfront Trail that will hug the Colorado River while joining the state parks system together into one walking/hiking network. Imagine being able to leisurely walk for over 40 miles along the riverfront of one of America's premier waterways, while gazing up at the spectacular Book Cliffs to the north, the Uncompahgre Plateau and the Colorado National Monument to the west, and the imposing Grand Mesa to the east. Here, city and nature merge, allowing people to always feel close to their natural heritage.

In Denver, the Highline Canal weaves its way through the city, a tree-lined waterway whose accompanying walking path allows the traveler to feel as if he or she is in the countryside, rather than in Colorado's largest city. City parks are abundant; so are bike paths and walking trails. The most visited state park, Cherry Creek, lies within the metropolitan area. This sprawling lake and nature preserve covers over 4,200 land and water acres, and joins the neighboring Chatfield State Park, with its 5,300 total acres—natural havens in the midst of Denver's booming urban development. Visitors to both parks can swim, sail, hike, fish, and camp, as if they were miles away in the Rocky Mountains.

Responsive and responsible city and state planning made this a reality. Five more state parks within 30 miles of downtown Denver make this area one of the most nature-accessible in the entire United States. From the corporate boardrooms, seminar and convention meeting rooms, college classrooms, offices, and businesses of Denver, residents and visitors alike are offered beautiful, enriching recreational outlets within minutes. The city has embraced its natural heritage. If Denver can do it, why not every urban area in the country?

Hiking!

The Ultimate Natural Prescription
for Health and Wellness

*"Climb the mountains and get their good tidings. Nature's
peace will flow into you as sunshine flows into trees, the
winds will blow their own freshness into you, and the storms
their energy, while cares will drop off like autumn leaves."*

—*John Muir,* "The Wilderness World of John Muir"

HIKING IS A HEALTHY LIFESTYLE
FOR TEENS TO SENIORS

The act of walking through nature affects people in a
holistic way: the complete human being receives some
benefit from hiking. The body receives a vigorous workout; the will is challenged to reach beyond itself when the
trail beckons up to steep mountain heights; the individual's
sense of responsibility grows with the successful planning
and execution of any trip logistics; personal connections
take place between hikers sharing their concerns, hopes,
and challenges; and the spirit is refreshed by the beauty of
unpretentious nature. Even though hiking is thought to
be the simplest of activities, all the simplicities of a hike

work together in a complex whole to create wellness for body, soul, heart, and spirit.

Hiking is an activity that helps produce "wellness" in the person practicing it. Our physical, mental, psychological, social, creative, and spiritual needs are, in part, fulfilled by a regular regimen of hiking. Ask hikers about the benefits of this "sport" or interest, and they have specific, enthusiastic, reasons why they hike, reasons that are connected to the fulfillment of real needs.

"I took up hiking when I was fifty-one," said a friend of mine. "I never thought that it would impact my life like it has; I never was the 'outdoor' type. Show me a corporate office, and I was home. But I was also greatly out of shape . . . a real mess sometimes. Part of me was actually afraid of being alone in nature. Nature was an unfamiliar place. I couldn't trust my body to take me where I wanted to go, certainly not to scramble over rocks and up mountainsides. But over the past several years I've become something of a mountain goat. My business friends from my pre-hiking days can hardly believe that I've hiked 11 miles and 8,000 feet straight up a mountain! Now I feel confident on the trail. I trust my conditioning, and I've learned that nature is a friendly place after all, especially if you're prepared and if you like being out in it."

Hiking greatly helps reduce stress and clarify thinking, assessment, and decision-making processes; it gives perspective on issues and concerns that a person needs to see clearly and from multiple points of view. Hiking can help you dramatically lose weight, firm and tone, build cardiovascular and aerobic conditioning, strengthen muscles, and energize your body at a very high level. Hiking guides a person into their own deeper self, into a healthier connection and friendship with who they really are; in the process, it helps free people from dependency and negative conditioning, feelings, or ideas, and instead reveals the great spiritual lessons and divine presence found throughout the natural world. Solitude becomes a friend; honest, quality sharing with a loved one can be greatly enhanced. Hiking provides a setting to enhance relationships, build intimacy, more closely bond with someone, facilitate communications with hiking companions, and meet and get to know new friends, while gaining a deeper sense of oneness with all humanity and all life on our planet.

Hikers gain self-confidence about their ability to move about successfully and safely in the natural world. Hiking allows the opportunity to teach, share with, and enjoy children in ways not possible in the more competitive society we live in. It offers a means of gaining a peaceful and quiet retreat from the onslaughts of media and modern culture while offering an endless flow of beautiful scenery, which inspires deep creative urgings and brings joy not commonly found anywhere else. Hiking, in some very special and private moments, provides the setting in which the deity of your own heartfelt personal experiences can reach out and touch your soul with a kind love and guidance that are reflected throughout all the glories of creation.

Hiking enlivens both body and soul, heart and mind, offering the best in the human experience to anyone willing to venture out along the trail, alone or with friends and family. For some, this lifelong adventure has already begun the day they took their first hike. For many more of us, the trail still beckons for the first time.

HIKING BALANCES MENTAL AND PHYSICAL ACTIVITY AND REDUCES STRESS

With so many demands on a person's time in modern living (or surviving!), it behooves a person to honestly evaluate the multitude of pulls and tugs that assault the individual each day, every day, throughout the day. In prioritizing, a person needs to ask him or herself what he or she does on a daily and weekly basis that has real value. What really fulfills, meets real needs, and responds to one's deeper strivings? Hiking can come high on the list of those activities that actually deliver the "goods."

Chapters 3, Psychology of Hiking, and 4, Stress Management and Hiking, emphasize the profound psychological benefits of hiking. Walking through nature gives a person perspective on their life, their problems, opportunities, pending life changes, concerns, challenges. Solutions arise out of their own self-dialogue, as they ramble over the countryside, free from the pressing reminders of society, obligations, and consumption marketing.

The father of Teddy Roosevelt recognized that his son possessed a sharp, inquisitive mind but lacked a strong body to support that intelligence. He encouraged Teddy to develop his physical well-being and overall health to balance and energize his mental prowess. Roosevelt did it by combining gym workouts with a lifetime of devotion to the outdoors through hiking, boating, and horseback riding. Teddy's success as a great human being was in part due to this balancing of his physical well-being with his mental, creative self. Both aspects were in harmony.

Hiking reduces stress, helps a person let go of excessive, negative thoughts and repressed emotions, while helping the individual feel relaxed and energized after every hike. Most hikers I've talked to report that upon returning home after a day on the trail, they experience a general sense of well-being. They feel calmer, more relaxed, confident, having accomplished something with real value for themselves. They have promoted their own wellness by the simple act of walking into and through nature. Hiking with few time constraints truly is a natural remedy for human wellness.

The effects of a hike, depending on where you live in America, might look something like this. You prepare all the necessary equipment, food, and clothing, hop in the car, and drive to the trailhead. Before reaching your destination, the soothing effects of going on a hike are already felt. Those problems at work, that concern about a relationship, the confrontation with someone earlier in the week—all fade in importance as the beautiful scenery of the open countryside passes by. Once you reach the trailhead, the anticipation of the day's adventure takes over, augmented by the exhilaration of being outside. The grasses, plant life, and forests are sweet; the clean air excites the senses. You begin to reconnect to your physical self, celebrating the senses and your experience of them.

As the hike progresses, the exertion of your body going uphill, walking through the invigorating air, releasing all its tensions, fills you with energy. Your step quickens, you feel glad for having taken this hike, now, on this day. Your body talks to you, letting you know that it is part of your extended self. If you are properly conditioned, there is little real strain. Instead, you feel more alive with each step. It's fun, an adventure encountering nature on its own terms, discovering new scenes of restful beauty.

With each hike, the hiker rediscovers his or her roots in the natural world. Witnessing the flow and change of the seasons reminds us of the flow of our own lives, and the hope and promise that come with spring and summer. We taste cool water, smell fragrant plants, visually marvel at soaring cloud formations building over majestic mountains, and feel connected once again to our own body and the physical universe that gave it birth. We feel "home" again.

HIKING IS COMPLETE AND NATURAL EXERCISE

Hiking has two aspects: the actual brisk movement through nature known as hiking, and the experience of nature through which the hiker moves, as we shall see in chapter 5, Physical Benefits of Hiking.

Every day people go into sports clubs and gyms to work out and exercise. They walk past the front desk, show their membership cards, climb aboard a stairstep machine or treadmill, or begin circuit weight training, then exchange one set of machines for another. In less than an hour they have exercised, sweated, burned a few calories. Perhaps it was an aerobics class they attended, or a jog around the indoor track. Whatever it was, they got what they came for, then left. A sometimes noisy environment, with odors of sweat and athletic clothes, often without sunlight or just a minimal amount, maybe with some socializing but mostly an in-and-out experience—health clubs are too often extensions of the cities surrounding them, enclosed rather than open, mechanical rather than natural.

Contrast this with a group of friends or fellow hikers joined together for a two- or three-hour hike along some forest, mountain, or desert trail. The feeling is of freedom: freedom from the city, the noise, the smells, the crowds, the enclosed horizons. The setting is open: openness to the four horizons, the sky, the clouds, the rolling hills, prairie, mountain valleys, the person next to you on the trail, and especially yourself. The inspiration is beauty: the beauty of the green pine, birch, aspen, fir, or redwood trees, reaching upward toward a river of white clouds swirling across the expansive azure sky; the land beautiful with purple, gray, and red-hued mountains, or camel, rust, burnt magenta, or snow-white sand or soil filling the wide, inviting valleys between a thousand variations of mountain, plateau, mesa, and hills. The smell is of blue-green sage, heavy in the desert stillness after the spring rain or in the early morning humidity, the delight of pine, or fresh blossoming flowers rising from the sweet prairie, or wildflowers flowing effortlessly, like a river of color, down a dark green Colorado, Washington, Montana, or Appalachian mountainside. The feelings are peaceful: feelings of restful stillness broken only by the wind sweeping down the mountains, stirring the trees, caressing the grasslands; warm feelings of joy that come from being reborn again in the welcomed presence of the Creator's handiwork, the Great Park made for humans known as "Nature."

Hiking is natural. We use the same walking motion to hike that we use to walk from any one destination to another—but there are no additives, preservatives, or chemicals present. Instead, the sweet-scented, clear air of nature's grasses, forests, cool mountains, meadows, salt-sprayed seashores, or life-filled riparian wetlands replaces the stale, gas- and diesel-choked, smog- and factory-filled atmospheres of modern urban areas. Air enriched with oxygen pouring forth from millions of plants offers a welcomed change from city odors.

Hiking relaxes us and promotes total health and fitness, while toning the body and encouraging weight loss or maintenance. A moderate 10-mile hike with several hours of ascent helps the average person burn 1,600 calories; hike up a steeper mountain slope, and benefit from the equivalent of several hours on a stairstepper. Hiking offers an excellent aerobic conditioning for the body, strengthening the legs, toning and firming, releasing pent-up stress in constricted muscles. Weight loss, muscle toning, aerobic conditioning, and a raised metabolic rate—just from taking a hike!

HIKING BUILDS COMMUNITY AND RELATIONSHIPS

In chapters 6, The Hiking Community, and 7, Romance on the Trail we discover that hiking in the company of good friends, enjoying fresh air and beautiful scenery, encourages a noncompetitive social experience with open exchanges between hikers. Needs for social interaction and sensory stimulation can be met through the safe, effective, and fun activity known as hiking. Hiking promotes family togetherness away from crowded cities and distracting television, teaches our children positive values as we experience nature, and hiking is an activity that can be enjoyed at any age.

I have taken children ages six, seven, eight, and older on hikes and seen their faces fill with wonder as we explored caves, examined wildflowers, crossed rivers, and trekked through wonder-filled rain forests. Their boundless energy, mixed with youthful curiosity, found more than ample expression on a hike. Parents find that children who have an average degree of self-discipline readily take to hiking.

Teens are constantly in need of "healthy outlets" in a world that does not yet recognize their adulthood. In the physical exercise that hiking offers, teens find an excellent channel for their raised levels of energy, their need for legitimate challenges, and a noncompetitive social interaction that raises self-esteem rather than threatens it. I've taken teens on many hikes where their expansive curiosity about nature and its plant and animal populations were well satisfied. After a 10-mile day hike, many young people often expressed appreciation for a day well spent. Fifteen-year-old Robert exclaimed after his first hike, "I never thought I could hike six miles and enjoy it so much. Can we go again next week-end?"

For adults in their twenties and thirties, hiking is an inexpensive hobby or pastime that allows them to "see the world" as they discover the natural heritage America is so endowed with. The canyonlands of Utah, the high alpine mountain trails of the Rockies, Sierras, Cascades, Sawtooths, and Appalachian Mountains, and the coasts and forests across the nation give young people living in the nearby urban areas a playground that heals, rejuvenates, de-stresses, excites, stimulates, and inspires—just by hiking into these wonderlands.

People in their early adult years benefit greatly from the moderate cost of weekend or vacation-length hiking trips. Singles can meet in the more informal experience of a hiking club, nature group, conservation outing, or service trip to repair or build trails; just take a hike or share one's love of the outdoors with someone with a similar bent. And the exercise afforded by hiking gives young adults a consistent, more easily followed exercise regimen that is more fun and stimulating than trips to the gym.

Couples find that hiking together is a natural way to share feelings, perceptions, philosophies, and values, or to express needs or concerns that often get buried or forgotten back home. Hiking offers couples the uninterrupted togetherness and meaningful companionship that marriage counselors claim is so necessary for love to flourish. Sharing in the beauty of nature has a way of giving perspective to couples who sometime take their own point of view too seriously, while reminding them of things whose value endures.

With the growing trend of working at home, hiking offers the flexible "new entrepreneur" the opportunity to take an exercise break on their terms. Alone, with a hiking buddy or friends, going out into nature and hiking offers someone the chance to socialize, receive and give creative feedback and re-energize without worrying about a tee time, an open court or freed up equipment at the gym. Hiking enhances this and any other lifestyle by helping to "simplify" one's life, uncluttering it in favor of quiet and clarifying moments on the trail. A businessman I know who is self-employed observed that "hiking has allowed me the freedom to recharge my batteries in a stress-free activity that gives me something to look forward to during the work week, something easy to do, uncomplicated and fun. I simply make a hiking date with a friend and take to the local hills. Being out of town, away from my work for a few hours gives me just the activity I need to return to my work revitalized."

Middle-aged adults discover hiking to be a "second childhood." Those who are too busy raising kids, career climbing, or simply just surviving find that hiking allows them to "play outside" again, to discover the centering power of the earth and the inspirational spirituality of tranquil beauty. They often reconnect with nature after years of neglecting it. Hiking is a form of exercise less damaging to joints, knees, and old injuries, yet gives a complete aerobic and toning workout.

Hiking offers seniors beyond age sixty the opportunity to practice an exercise program that is kind to their bodies while still providing all the benefits of rigorous exercise. It also gives seniors something stimulating to do with their free time. There are so many trails to discover, enjoy, and explore, in so many different regions of both our own country and others. Hiking offers travel, companionship, and educational opportunities not only for retirees, but for people throughout their lifespan.

Because hiking is an outdoor activity/pastime almost anyone can enjoy, hiking offers benefits to all generations. William Strauss and Neil Howe, in *The Fourth Turning* identify and name several contemporary generations which are each benefited by the positive effects of hiking.

The Generation-X or 13ers (born between 1961-81) will find hiking an inexpensive challenge that can be spontaneously done almost any time of year. Hiking remains an inexpensive pastime, offering as much adventure as anyone might care to pursue, from hiking "fourteeners" in Colorado to crossing the great expanses of Utah and Arizona's Colorado Plateau.

The Boomers (1943–60) will be especially pleased to discover how hiking responds to many needs and attitudes unique to their generation. Their spiritual/values quest will be supported by hiking into the meaningful beauty of nature, uncovering the honest simplicity found there.

Traveling into and through nature, the wilderness, spending a day, week-end or more in reflection, listening to the stirrings of *their own souls* rather than the media-offered truths of the 20th century, boomers will flourish and heal in nature's nourishment of the human heart and spirit—connected to the timeless truths of the greater "Spiritual Innernet." Hiking as a family, children along to share in the adventure of discovering nature, can only strengthen family values, bring families together, create a community of nature lovers with both relatives and friends, and offer opportunities to deepen character and build virtue.

The members of the Silent Generation (1925–1942) will find mixing with the young along the trail revitalizing. This generation will be able to continue fostering the close relationships they so dearly prize by hiking with both their children, grandchildren and with parents who still enjoy the pleasures of the outdoors. They will reclaim "childhood" once again, as they stay involved, active, healthy and still "learning" while perhaps pursuing a pastime never before enjoyed or reclaimed after years of parental and work responsibilities.

The G.I. Generation (1901-1924) will field members of their age group that still exalt in their ability to walk the wilderness, riverpaths or country roads. Indeed a handful already celebrate birthdays by hiking the Grand Canyon or climbing Mt. Whitney. No challenge too late or too great!

HIKING INSPIRES CREATIVITY AND SPIRITUALITY

As we will see in chapters 8, Hiking and Creativity, and 9, The Spirituality of Hiking, weekly hikes in the outdoors—

where no urban reminders weigh us down, where just trees, mountains, grasslands, rivers, and lakes envelop and comfort the visitor, helping people to re-create their lives with more balance and peace—is the one sure way that we can rediscover our gentler, kinder nature. Our roots in the natural world offer us a deeper connection with the best in our human nature and the spiritual world that surrounds us.

Hiking is a vital means toward achieving these life-enhancing goals, a natural prescription for promoting health and wellness. The spiritual uplift that nature brings and its creative inspirations are found when we hike. The soul is nourished by the beauty of nature, its simplicity, accessibility, unconditionality. Creativity is enhanced; aesthetic needs are met.

During the course of a hike, especially one that is taken alone, the individual often finds that by not having to deal with the world, he or she can begin listening to inner voices of inspiration, wisdom, and personal destiny. Authors, artists, businesspeople, and others have told me of their experiences of creativity while hiking—a new solution to an old problem, a new way of looking at something. The energy released while hiking combines with a creative flow from deep within our more "true self" and supports our efforts to return to our lives with new resolve and a fresh perspective, perhaps new goals and projects closer to our needs and abilities.

DAYHIKING: HOW TO GET STARTED

A good dayhike requires awareness, planning, decisions, discipline, and a positive attitude. You've got to recognize the conditions of the season you're in. If it's too hot at a lower elevation, hike a trail higher up. Are there insects you might encounter, enough that some trails are best left for another time of year? How much snow is at the higher elevations? Will you be prepared with the equipment you're bringing? If it's wildflowers you want to see, where are the best trails to view them?

A successful hike is mostly comfortable, safe, and enjoyable. But achieving these results requires proper equipment, safety gear, enough food and drink, and of course the right footwear. These basics are discussed briefly below; in addition, consult some of the many fine hiking guides that can introduce you to the basics of hiking. *Wilderness Basics*, by the San Diego chapter of the Sierra Club (The Mountaineers, 1993) is a complete handbook for dayhikers as well as backpackers. *A Hiker's Companion* by Cindy Ross and Todd Gladfelter (The Mountaineers, 1993) offers 12,000 miles of trail-tested wisdom. These are just a couple of suggestions; also check your local outdoor gear store or library.

Equipment
Comfortable and safe equipment begins with footwear and finding properly fitting boots. On easy trails, good supportive tennis or walking shoes might be all you need. However, most hikers "graduate" to moderate and strenuous trails where safe hiking requires that footwear provide protection for your soles from the pounding they might take from rocks, and lateral support is given to avoid twisted ankles and sprains. Boots for dayhiking should be both light and strong. Dayhiking boots are often a combination of leather and a light fabric, such as cordura.

Your boot should fit comfortably, with adequate toe room so as to avoid jamming your toes against the front of your boot when going downhill, and space enough to accommodate the swelling of your feet that comes after several hours of hiking. For this reason, it is best to get a fitting for boots in the late afternoon when your feet might be as swelled as they are going to get for a day, thereby approximating the swelling that would take place on the trail.

Next to boots, socks are one of the most important pieces of clothing hikers must consider. Hiking socks are most supportive and comfortable when they are padded at the ball of the foot and at the heel. The material should be thicker than ordinary athletic socks and composed of a combination synthetic material and wool or acrylic. Underneath your socks it is also helpful to wear a polypropylene sock liner that helps keep your feet dry and comfortable.

Because hiking generates a rise in body heat and sweat, depending on the temperature and humidity, you must wear clothes that keep you dry, comfortable, protected from wind and the elements, and adequately insulated. Dress in "layers." This means wearing next to your skin a material that conveys sweat away from the skin and onto an outer layer. A possible lightweight material such as polypropylene works well. The middle layer, if cold and wet weather is part of the hiking conditions, should be a thicker polyester material known as fleece or pile, usually in the form of a jacket or pullover. Finally, a wind and waterproof jacket or shell should be worn, such as Gore-Tex, that also allows moisture to escape to the garment's outer surface.

For desert or warm weather conditions, a lightweight synthetic T-shirt, shorts, or nylon polyester pants suffice. However, since rain is always a consideration, unless hiking during a desert dry season, a waterproof poncho or other outer protection is also advisable. A lightweight, broad-brimmed hat protects from sunburn, while a knit cap insulates the head from loss of body heat in colder weather, and for fair-skinned hikers, a lightweight long-sleeved shirt is good sun protection.

Dayhikers require a pack of some sort to store food, drink, equipment, clothes, etc. Daypacks are light and far less bulky than backpacks. Two styles now in use include the pack that secures around the waist, known as a "fanny pack," and a pack that is secured with straps over the shoulder. Be sure that the way your waterbottles are carried in the pack is the way you like. Some packs allow waterbottles to fit into "pockets" on the outside of the pack, others allow you to fit bottles inside the pack. A third option is to carry your drink in a special "camel-pack," a kind of large pack that straps over the shoulders and has storage space for placing bladderlike drink containers.

Basic items that hikers should take with them to insure safety and comfort, sometimes called the Ten Essentials include: 1. Adequate food. 2. Extra clothing, including rain gear. 3. Pocket Knife. 4. First aid kit. 5. Matches, in a weatherproof container. 6. Sunglasses. 7. Compass. 8. Fire-starting material. 9. Flashlight, with extra batteries. 10. Map of the hike you plan and of the immediate area.

Depending on the weather and season, you might have to also take extra warm clothing, extra water or drink, especially if doing a desert hike during the warm season, sunscreen, bug repellent, and extra food if the hike is especially long or strenuous.

Food for dayhikes should lean toward carbohydrates for needed energy such as fruit, both fresh and dry, crackers, trail mixes, various energy bars on the market, nuts, cheese, bread, candy bars, etc. Water seems to be the drink of choice for dayhikers, but other liquids are also available. Sports drinks give both electrolyte replenishment and added carbohydrates for energy. In warm climates try freezing half your drink in your drink bottle and, on the morning of the hike, fill the remaining portion with cold liquid. You will have a cool drink during most if not the entire hike.

The most important drink consideration is the amount. As a rule, take one quart for every 5 miles hiked, and an additional quart if the temperature is near 90 degrees or the weather is overly humid. Although you might not be thirsty, because the thirst mechanism in the body tends to kick in late rather than early, make sure you drink what you bring in regular, spaced amounts. Rehydrating your body this way gives you additional stamina and avoids the possibility of heatstroke.

Safety
What are the safety considerations for a typical hike? Let's go through an entire "hike sequence" to discover what safety measures one might take to insure both safety and comfort.

Weather check: What is the forecast for both temperature and weather? Dress accordingly, take the proper amounts of drink, rain gear, etc. Pack extra clothing if a chance of snow or cold temperatures exist.

Notification: Tell someone where you are going and when you plan to return. If something happens to you on the trail, it's comforting to know that someone knows where you are and when you planned to return.

Hike selection: Pick a hike to match your physical conditioning and ability. Make sure you have a map of where you are going, and some idea of what the trail is like. If you've never climbed over 1,000 feet in elevation gain, don't choose a trail that has a 3,000-foot elevation gain.

Take a friend: On easy hikes into areas that are well traveled, going alone is not such a serious consideration. But when doing more moderate and certainly strenuous hikes, hike with at least one other person. If one of you gets into trouble requiring outside assistance, the other person can go for help. Traveling in a group of three is even better— one to stay with a possible injured hiker and the other to go for help. Most people who hike alone usually do so only after becoming experienced enough to deal with emergency situations that might arise.

On the trail: Stay on the marked trail, both for safety and to prevent erosion. If you need to use nature's bathroom, leave the trail only after telling others, while they should remain close by, instead of continuing on without you. Stop at trail junctions to wait for all other hikers. Note the landmarks on or near the trail; if you get disoriented, you will at least have some memorized reference points to guide you. Practice this same technique even if someone else is acting as the leader or guide. If something should happen to them, you are still, and always responsible for your own safety and for knowing where you are.

Stream crossing: Avoid crossing fast-running streams that are at or above the knees. Just hike along the river or stream until you come to a safe crossing. Usually whatever agency is responsible for trail maintenance will have built log or other kinds of bridges for a safe crossing. Use a hiking stick or a makeshift staff, or the support of a friend, to help you across. Some waterways in late spring can be nothing but ice-cold snowmelt; staying too long in this low temperature water could bring on other health threats.

Adverse weather: If you've taken the proper gear, you'll be able to weather most conditions. But if conditions become more severe than you're prepared for, turn back or seek shelter, usually in a thick wood. In a lightning storm, avoid exposed areas, open areas, and ridges. The shelter of thick woods might be the safest place. The effects of a cold wind can be minimized by having the proper clothing, a good insulating windbreaker, and warmer clothes underneath. If you lose heat too rapidly, you risk hypothermia, which can lead to serious injury. Be prepared is simply the best rule to follow. Wear a hat that will stay on during stiff wind gusts, such as a stocking cap, or a hat secured with a leather strap that you can tie underneath your chin.

Animals: Avoid wild animals of any kind. Do not attempt to "get in closer" for a photo op. Respect wild animals, their home territory, and how they perceive humans. A rule of thumb about snakes is don't put your hands in places where you can't see what's there, e.g., under logs, rocks, etc. Look where you're stepping and be aware of your surroundings at all times.

Altitude: Hiking in elevations above 6,000 to 8,000 feet could cause difficulties for some individuals. Less oxygen and lower humidity sometimes causes altitude sickness, a condition that produces shortness of breath, headaches, insomnia, poor digestion, fatigue, and dizziness. Acclimate to higher elevation before any strenuous exercise or hiking. Even after adjusting to the higher altitude, hikes which climb considerably to altitudes above 10,000 feet require the hiker to conserve energy (do not attempt to "run" up the mountain), rest, drink plenty of fluids, and turn back if experiencing serious difficulty. If you think you are experiencing altitude sickness, go to lower elevation immediately. Prolonged symptoms can lead to serious, even fatal illness.

Bites, stings, and poisonous plants: Ticks often cling to the tips of low-lying plants. Some protection is afforded by insect repellent. Wear light clothing; hikers should check each other every mile or so, in the hair, on the clothing, and in soft areas of the skin. Ticks can cause itching and sometimes a raised rash that subsides in three to four days.

Poison ivy, poison oak, and other irritant, oily plants can cause severe itching, accompanied by a raised rash. Learn to identify these plants and avoid them. By walking on the trail, and not into the nearby brush, you can generally avoid this menace. If any discomfort caused by tick bites, poison ivy, or other bites or stings persists, consult your physician.

Trail Etiquette
Perhaps the number-one point of etiquette during a hike is to keep the trail clean. Whatever you pack in, take out with you. This includes paper, plastic, and glass of any kind.

Trails are built to assist water runoff and to be minimal in affecting erosion. Stay on the trail rather than cut across country.

Respect the silence of the wilderness. Where trail use is heavy even during a dayhike, speak in civil tones, rather than loud, boisterous, or argumentative conversations. Leave anger at home, and instead let the peace of the wilderness replace it.

When breaking for lunch, a snack, etc., rest away from the trail, rather than make other hikers move around you on the trail. Stand to one side of the trail to allow other trail traffic—mountain bikers, joggers, and equestrians—

pass you. It's just easier for someone on foot to ease off the trail than to manage a horse or mountain bike.

Tips for the Trail
When planning a hike, especially with other hikers, give yourself plenty of time to finish your hike before feeling obligated to return to civilization for some command performance, duty, or volunteered service. It's not fair to yourself, and your hiking companions will grow weary of your complaints about not making it to your appointment on time.

Choose your hiking companions wisely. Avoid people trying to do business on the trail, or people who hike in a very different style from yours. If you like to hike fast, go with fast hikers, not someone who likes to stop and smell the flowers or examine every little highlight the trail offers. And slower hikers who enjoy a more leisure strolling pace should likewise choose fellow travelers who enjoy taking their time. If the group is large enough to accommodate multiple hiking speeds and styles, no one should complain about anyone else's hiking manner.

While hiking, listen to your body! If you find yourself hiking several miles of straight up trail, then take time out to rest more often. Hiking is not a time trial event. Use generous rest stops and a slower pace on strenuous hikes. When your body tells you to slow down or rest—listen to it.

Even with great preparation and equipment, you need a responsible attitude. No whiners! You've got to "decide" to go, arrive in a timely fashion, enjoy yourself, and return while the lighting and the gear you brought insure your safety.

Gaining Experience

People who have been hiking for years rarely think about what constitutes a good hike. They just do it. They come properly prepared, in all aspects. They have learned the "program" of successful hiking, just like an enjoyable camping trip that requires many "little" things to be done before the trip becomes successful. Responsible preparation, coupled with a good attitude, are the keys to enjoyable hiking.

If you seldom hike or have never hiked, ask a hiker the benefits he or she receives from walking nature's countless byways. Hike with such a person to gain valuable experience. Or consider hiking with an organization such as those described in chapter 6, The Hiking Community. There are suggestions for places to go hiking in chapter 10, The Dayhiking Vacation. And when you do strike out on your own for a day "out there," and assess the outcome after such an adventure, the verdict hopefully will come in as an honest affirmation of the great benefits of hiking. After each hike, assess how you feel, what benefits you gained from the experience. There is nothing to lose by challenging this activity for its own merits, and there is so much to gain when you find how much health and wellness flows out of a hiking lifestyle.

Hiking is, in a real sense, an ultimate and complete "natural remedy" for promoting and maintaining health and wellness—nature itself is the tonic. It addresses a wide variety of human needs in such a way that those who hike experience a total kind of well-being, delivered in the most pleasing of ways. Hiking is great fun; ask anyone who has trekked through desert and over plateaus, up mountains and along sea coasts, through forests and across prairies.

Throughout the rest of this book, each chapter describes in detail the ways in which hiking meets our various human needs. Chapter 11, Building the Future, gives hikers some suggestions for giving back to the natural world to which we turn for rejuvenance. In the back of the book, you'll find a sampler of a few hiking clubs, some inspiring places to go to hike, and addresses for some of the agencies that manage these lands.

However, no amount of discussion or reading "about" hiking and nature will yield the rich treasures gained from just one hike into the wilderness. Hiking must be experienced to be known and, being known, fulfills many of our deepest needs. Accept the invitation of famed naturalist John Muir when he wrote "the clearest way into the universe is through a forest wilderness." If that is true, then this book is the perfect companion to help you find your way.

Listen to and walk out into the world our ancestors first discovered, the world of the high and majestic mountains, the bountiful lowland valleys, the cool, green hills of earth, the welcoming, scented forests, windswept prairies, calming lakes and rivers and streams, expansive mesas and plateaus, intricate canyons, cloud-filled skies, and canopy of the universe above in the black stillness of night, where the stars, like dust, reach out, a river of light offering us the promise of love's inspiration from the creator into whose world hiking has taken us: home again.

A PHILOSOPHY OF HIKING

The Values of
Outdoor Recreation

"The longest journey is the journey inwards. Of him who has chosen his destiny, who has started upon his quest for the source of his being. The more faithfully you listen to the voice within you, the better you will hear what is sounding outside. And only he who listens can speak. Is this the starting point of the road towards the union of your two dreams—to be allowed in clarity of mind to mirror life and in purity of heart to mold it?"

—*Dag Hammarskjold,* Markings *(1964)*

HIKING AS A METAPHOR FOR LIFE AND LIVING

Life has often been compared to a journey, a movement through time and human experiences from birth to death. Hiking is also a movement, the individual moving through nature, overland. And if no one ventured out to and through nature, what would humanity lose? What do we gain when we make this journey through forests, valleys, canyons, over hills, mesas, plateaus and mountains?

Hiking offers humanity an option for a kind of "time out;" hiking can take us momentarily out of our culture. When do we take time off from cultural conditioning? When do we confront life as a deeper reality, where individually we struggle with the meaning of "our" life? When do we examine the value and happiness of our lives as a reflection of how spiritual, human, loving, alive, aware, vital, enthusiastic, courageous, creative, and serving we've become?

Hiking can be our entree into the sanctuary of our own hearts and souls. In this out-in-nature solitude we can begin to rediscover ourselves and the priorities that often become buried by the demands of life lived in reaction to culture. Solitude itself becomes a much needed respite, a "re-creational" experience that helps us build and care for our very souls.

Besides leaving our culture, during a hike we also loosen our attachment to the roles, expectations, rules, and limitations that so often define our life. Out in nature, just for a while, and especially if we hike alone, we stand clear of every "paradigm" we "belong to and participate in"—our jobs, our relationships, where we live, what organizations and groups we function in. On a mountain trail, in a desert canyon, on a sweeping prairie, or along an expansive seashore—alone, we seem to gain a perspective free from our involvement in this life. In nature we can more clearly see ourselves, what we react to, and what our real issues are. The garments of culture fall from our shoulders—we are left facing the simpler reality known as nature.

But Americans don't totally trust the idea of solitude. We appreciate the romance of Thoreau's life at Walden Pond, but tend to think of him as having been a tad eccentric. C. Anthony Starr underscored this notion when he says

"People achieve conventional success at the expense of inner development. . . . We need to pay attention to the positive internal changes that occur during solitude." Hiking, in its simplicity, counters the trend of technological overload by offering people the means of tuning out the chaos, noise, and clamor of the modern world, in favor of listening, in that space of solitude, to our own deeper selves, and to the quiet truths that nature presents.

SANCTUARY FROM THE "NEW CITY"

No longer does the physical encroachment of the city alone assault our senses, but now anywhere on the planet, through the medium of electronic gadgetry like cell phones and fax machines, individuals carry in their head this "new city," through telecommunications. Ours is an addictive society, bent on reacting fast and furious to whatever momentarily captures our fancy or stimulates our inner emptiness. Many of us follow trends instead of following our own inner promptings and values. What is "in" is what can temporarily fill our emptiness, for awhile replacing what we have lost or never had: ourselves.

Solitude counters the tidal wave of cultural conditioning and distraction modern life serves up. Nature becomes in today's world what a church was in medieval times—a sanctuary. There is peace in nature; the natural world is just "there," unconditionally, without demands, expectations, or the ability to use the observer.

Americans are not accustomed to this lack of using something or someone. The "sale" is part of our psyche. All our institutions—educational, religious, business, government and politics, entertainment, and the media—have something to sell, something they want people to incorporate into their lives. Nature, however, reflects none of this. It simply is there to be experienced, enjoyed. It stands alone, in relationship to the observer as a friend would be, not trying to change us or gain advantage from us. And in this way of being and presenting itself, nature offers us the gift of peace and inner tranquillity.

The peace found on the trail yields other treasures as well. During a hike, the individual experiences the power and confidence that comes from giving themselves the gift of leisure and the time to enjoy it. It is this same lack of leisure time that is a symptom, not the cause, of our runaway lifestyles. Too often we have forgotten how to simply enjoy ourselves in the present moment; we have lost some of our precious freedom that comes not from learning what we can live with, but what we have learned to live without.

Dag Hammarskjold wrote, in *Markings*, "He came with his little girl. She wore her best frock. In the morning sunshine it had been festive. Now most people had gone home. So the place looked rather bleak and deserted when he came with his little girl to taste the joy of spring and warm himself in the freshly polished Easter sun. But she was happy. They both were. They had learned a humility. A humility which never makes comparisons, never rejects what there is for the sake of something 'else' or something 'more'."

What is the secret of their happiness and contentment? In the time they made for themselves to be alone, with the day unfolding itself and nature offering its simple presence, this father and daughter rested in the sanctuary of the present moment enfolding the fullness of each person.

To experience one's own loved and loving self is what a "whole self" knows as fulfillment. Individuals realize that well-being does not come from something outside themselves. There is nothing to chase. There is no "better" experience to be had next Saturday if only we wait for it to be offered to us. We can commit to being ourselves and being with ourselves . . . if we have lovingly accepted ourselves.

The stillness of nature offers people the opportunity to grasp and acknowledge these kinds of realities. Each and every scene along the trail is its own perfect picture, offering delights of color, sound, composition, and scent. Nature offers itself, as is. Like the experience of the father and the little girl on Easter, nature challenges us by just being there—which is enough.

UNIFYING BOTH SPONTANEOUS AND GOAL-DIRECTED BEHAVIOR

There are two approaches to living that people take: in one approach, people require a map with each possible experience along the way properly acknowledged and prepared for, and in the other approach, people begin a journey with adequate preparation but know little of what awaits them during the journey. These two approaches are termed goal-directed versus spontaneous behavior. Hiking mirrors these and accommodates both personal living styles, offering the sojourner the truth that in any life, as with any journey, both styles complement each other.

The goal-directed hiker would do well to remember that no amount of preparation can predict the subtle and often beautiful surprises found during any hike. Animals and birds suddenly appear on or near the trail; a once-cloudy, storm-threatening sky gives way to brilliant sunshine and warming temperatures. Hikers who plan their trip knowing what highlights the map shows cannot always account for the many beckoning side trips that certain rock outcroppings, generous flower displays, or serene meadow and stream settings surprise us with.

In the same vein, spontaneous hikers who only know where the trailhead is and set out to discover a certain trail for the first time would do well to understand the possible terrain difficulties, weather patterns for a given area, and physical difficulties of elevation gain and steepness that they might encounter.

Hiking encourages both of these approaches, and rewards each if they are practiced together. In fact, every personality style identified by psychologists finds in nature a home that accommodates their uniqueness. Nature accepts, rather than rejects.

LEARNING TO REALLY COMMUNICATE

We live in a hurried society. There seems to be less time for each other, as work and the demands of family claim large chunks of our free time. Seminars on "communication skills" abound, sold to people who have, ironically, relinquished to these seminars whatever free time they have left for communicating. Ours is a society filled with the technology of communication but not the will or the structure to actually communicate. We are still in need of that social institution that encourages and creates real face-to-face engagement between people, allowing us to discover each other free from pressure or expectation.

Hiking offers both the structure and the time for meaningful communication to flourish. During the many hikes I've been on, more than a few fellow hikers have shared their life story. Sometimes the issues of our times do arise, but are addressed in thought-provoking, insightful ways. Things go a lot deeper on the trail than surface chatter about the weather. The structure of two or more people in close contact with each other, with few if any distractions, and with the lack of any reminders of the dominant culture lends itself to people freely sharing life issues and concerns, feelings and reflections.

In these unhurried conversations, we gain valuable insight into ourselves, our attitudes, philosophies, values, and experiences. Another concerned human being next to us on the trail offers valued feedback, a chance for us to see things from more than just our perspective. During such sharings-along-the-way, I've discovered that hikers have learned something of our common needs, challenges, similarities, and differences. Hiking has enhanced our experience of being human. People have become less threatening, more familiar.

Hiking through nature sets the stage for this growth to take place. Being alone, or with just one other person or a few people, lowers our defenses, our need to protect ourselves from real or imaginary threats. The trail is friendly, nature is satisfying, the vistas are inspiring. In this positive, uplifting movement through nature—hiking—we have the opportunity to reach out to our fellow hiker and add to our lives in the process.

Hiking by its very nature promotes family togetherness. While on the trail, out in nature, or camping, there is freedom from the demands and expectations from other people, neighbors, or media distractions. Families have time to re-create together, to discover more of who one another are, to bond through the fun and nature-learning experiences that hiking offers whenever we visit the outdoors. The sharing that goes on between family members during a hike is easy, natural, and fun. It facilitates the intimacy of relationships that we need in our hurried world and lets us meet each other in a personal way free from roles or expectations. In nature we can all be kids again.

THE VALUE OF PREPARATION

Many daily activities teach us the value of adequate preparation, such as keeping the car properly oiled, our college and high school studies current, our diet, and our bodies exercised, etc. Hiking reinforces this value of good preparation in an often quick and direct way.

Hikers can get lost if they lack maps and the knowledge of where they are and where they are going. Weather can prove very uncomfortable if rain gear, proper clothing, and adequate water and food have been neglected. In the space of a few hours on the trail, the elements of nature can cause injury if they strike and the hiker is unprepared. Hiking constantly reinforces the need to pay attention to what we are doing and where we are going. Hiking encourages discipline, and discipline supports valuable personal growth.

In this light, hiking helps to build character. Hamlin Garland writes that "Do you fear the force of the wind? The slash of the rain? Go face them and fight them, be savage again. Go hungry and cold, like the wolf; go wade like the crane. The palms on your hands will thicken, the skin on your face will tan. You'll grow ragged and weary and swarthy, but you'll have walked like a man." Being lazy can prove hazardous to one's safety and well-being. Hiking is an experience that directly counters the numbing effects of excessive television watching and computer and video game use. A person "participates" in an involved, problem-solving way, both before and during a hike. The individual chooses and packs the gear, food, and clothing needed for a hike. If something is left out and this results in an uncomfortable experience on the trail (being in a cold rain shower with no rain gear, or running out of water on a desert hike when temperatures reach upward of 100 degrees), the hiker has no one to blame but him or herself. What allows someone to enjoy the beautiful passing scenery during a hike without much hassle is adequate preparation.

SELF-CONFRONTATION . . .
ALONE ON THE TRAIL

Technology, coupled with modern transportation and communication, pulls at our every free moment, offering us avenues of escape and distraction. As the Dag Hammarskjold quote at the beginning of this chapter notes, "The longest journey is the journey inwards." Many of us never really come to know ourselves, never honestly attempt the journey inward. We react. Opinion polls often express the perception of a leadership vacuum in the governing of the nation, which hints at more than just a lack of decision making. Perhaps we are also void of decision makers!

In a family I know, which has seven children, the wife expressed her concern to me that she feared for the success of her marriage when the last child was out of the home. Child rearing, it seemed, had occupied so much of their energies that they no longer knew one another. Modern times have taken a toll on more than parents. Singles often express the same need for self-discovery. There may be so many things to do, so little time to do them all, but the real challenge is for each individual to build a healthy relationship with themselves based on an honest self-awareness.

Alone on the trail, we are left to discover our self-confidence and tap into the familiar, hopefully loving relationship we've developed with ourselves. If we sense our anxiousness "out there," if fears well up and disturb our inner spirits, then at least we know that we have "work" to do in building a healthier sense of independence while addressing those fears.

Many hikers have shared with me the experience of feeling much more self-assured during a hike. It seems that in returning to civilization, we are reminded of the many "lacks" that media/advertising sometimes instill in us, while in nature we sense our own fullness and strength.

On the trail we almost naturally build self-confidence. Just by freeing ourselves from our immediate attachments and demands, we realize just how special and sacred we are. We've driven to the trailhead, brought the necessary provisions and equipment, taken to the hills, and proven "we can do it." Ask anyone who challenges themselves and their own aloneness, and most often they testify to having grown more whole from the experience.

FREEDOM FROM THE ARTIFICIAL

Children have long been admired for their spontaneous, natural responses of wonder, joy, and enthusiasm to the world unfolding around them. Adults bemoan this "loss of innocence" and seek nostalgic returns to simpler times. Yet there really doesn't have to be this innocence-gone-forever attitude in adults. Hiking brings the individual back to the natural world, a place free from the pressures of the marketplace, deadlines, and the ever-present encouragements to buy and "keep up."

There is a feeling of "time out" when hiking through nature. Each person can explore at their own pace, plod up a mountain slope or rest beside a cool meadow, responding to what they like rather than what someone else requires. Our time is once again ours. Physical space invites us to discover and explore as we see fit. We regain "control" over our lives in nature, recognizing that we ought to carry this personal power within us back to the cultural fray that we sometimes find life to be.

When we hike, then, we surrender much of what is not us and reclaim more of what and who we really are. Hiking and nature have combined to be the means of our welcomed "rebirth."

NATURE'S STOREHOUSE OF WISDOM

The word "philosophy" means the love of wisdom, of truth. Hikers over the ages have discovered that nature has its own way of showing visitors the truth and wisdom of its ways. One can read Muir or Thoreau or a host of other natural philosophers and glean the wisdom they have gained from years of studying nature. Better yet, one can experience nature on one's own and observe what nature can teach, inspired by the methods and ideas of these past philosophers. What each person finds is their own treasure of wisdom. But how to look and observe is a valuable tool in reaching these discoveries.

For example, walk out into an open space where mountains rise on some horizon. Go with no agenda in mind. I did this during a stressful time in my life one summer's day, walking out around a lake in Colorado, in the stretch of prairie just before coming to the Front Range of the Rocky Mountains. From the trail around the lake, I could look in all directions. To the east was endless prairie opening to a vast line of horizon. To the west was the long chain of Rocky Mountains, in front of which ran an equally long line of lower foothills stretching from the north in Wyoming toward where the lower foothills trailed off into smaller collections of hills lost in the curvature of the earth's slope toward the south.

Dark, threatening clouds were billowing over the mountains, but spaced so that clear skies could be seen at various intervals along the mountain front. Thunder and sheets of rain could be seen accenting these storms, while above me great swirling masses of clouds raced past, with huge gaps of sunshine and blue skies spaced in between.

While great conflicts were taking place in some parts of the sky and along the landscape and horizon, other parts enjoyed warm sunshine and clear sky. Nature's wisdom encouraged me to look at the conflicts I was experiencing in my own life, and I drew real comfort from the realization that if only I looked at the bigger picture, if only I looked with perspective on everything that was then happening to me, I would find strength, tranquillity, and rest in those areas of my life not engaged in these particular life battles. Nature had shown me underlying calm in the midst of the storm. It was now up to me to discover my underlying calm in my own life.

As if to press home this lesson, as the wind swept the lake from the different directions the storms were taking and the waters in those windy areas were choppy and swirling, I noticed that, miraculously, there were also parts of the lake as smooth as glass. Within my own soul, then, I might also find still waters and strength untouched by the conflicts that raged nearby—if only I would look more closely into my soul. Doing so, I soon found the inner peace that nature had suggested was there all along.

This is just one example of how a hike into nature can yield wisdom for living one's life more effectively and fully. But as with every school and course of study, it remains up to each individual to hike out into nature's "university" and look for its teachings, listen to its wisdom, and apply what we find to whatever in our lives needs positive change or healing. In deserts, in forests, alongside streams, rivers, and lakes, on mountainsides and peaks, or in the open spaces of prairie—nature's wisdom awaits our discovery, unlocked in part by the gentle effort of hiking.

THE PSYCHOLOGY OF HIKING

Building the
Total Person

"What you have to attempt—to be yourself.
What you have to pray for—to become a mirror in which,
according to the degree of purity of heart you have attained,
the greatness of life will be reflected."

—*Dag Hammarskjold,* Markings

Every human act has the potential to shape a person's mind and emotions through its own unique "psychology," defined in this sense as the capacity of an act to effect change, either negative or positive. Hiking, too, has a psychology. It affects the individual in a total, uplifting manner, and it does its almost magical work without fanfare.

Researchers for years have pursued the secrets of longevity. Have their findings yielded complex discoveries? Hardly. They have found that the simple acts of sleeping eight hours daily; eating balanced, low-fat, high-fiber meals; exercising regularly; not smoking; drinking moderately if at all; and getting preventive check-ups adds ten years to a person's lifespan. A "healthy" simplicity is the key to good health.

Science has also found that the most comprehensive, profound theories explaining the laws of the universe are to be had in those that are the least complex, the simplest . . . formulas that can be written in the confines of a short sentence. Getting back to the basics, yields the surest pathways to personal well-being.

Hiking is no different. The very simplicity of hiking is a powerful reason why this activity so positively impacts the human psyche. Taking to the trail frees you from the confines of daily routine, pulls you away from the demands of civilization. You know that an adventure awaits you from the first step, be it through sandy wastes, carpeted forests, or mountainous terrain. Energy begins flowing through you, along with fresh air and the joy of being surrounded by the aesthetic, spiritual powers of earth and sky. In nature we feel at home.

Our well-being is enhanced by the spiritual power of nature's vastness—the great empty expanses of the desert southwest with its plateau and mesa monuments, or Rocky Mountain ridges separating green oceans of alpine valleys—and by nature's simplicity, from the smallest leaf or fragile wildflower. Beauty, the spiritual calm that nature inspires, through the medium of the colorful canvas of earth tones, desert pastels of sunsets-in-sandstone, azure skies, deep purple mountains clad in purifying white snows—-all reach out and revitalize our psyches while returning the individual self to a more optimistic, childlike state of grace. Walking, climbing, scrambling, ascending, and descending all increase the body's vitality.

HIKING CONNECTS MIND AND BODY

We live in a passive society, a culture of images, sound-bites, and infomercials. Education often supports our marketing-oriented society by teaching young people how to access information via computers, the Internet, and television. Education sometimes fails, however, to teach skills that the individual can apply to assess, evaluate, or analyze this information barrage. People seldom learn how to relate one piece of information to another so that it helps the individual satisfy some of his or her basic needs.

People are encouraged to become passive observers, reactors to information rather than true processors of information. This American cultural bias has severely impacted our psyche. We have become less reflective and able to solve problems. The content of culture has often become too contrived and artificial. The everyday world is taking the human out of being human, draining our spirits and stressing our psyches. We have become divorced from our true and best selves, and from the natural world from where we once came.

Hiking is a tool that counteracts these harmful trends by restructuring a person's lifestyle so that he or she begins to grow more healthy and balanced. The physical intensity of this outdoor exercise helps the individual to reconnect body to soul by enlivening both. After most hikes, I experience a deep sense of aliveness, having become more aware of the natural world around me and my body's newfound energy through the heightening of my five senses. I've observed colorful scenes, smelled pine, sage, or flowers, touched cool mountain streams, tasted their waters, listened to the sounds of animals, storms, rivers, and rain.

Hiking is a vigorous form of exercise without resembling an intense hour's workout in the gym. A four- to five-hour hike, especially if it includes some uphill walking, helps release a great amount of tension and stress, but more importantly, it creates energy. Once created, this dynamic energy flows in the body, and helps bring the mind's awareness to the physical world. We become grounded in the simple power of our own self.

Hikers reconnect their mind with their body and its five senses. Since nature is a very sensual experience filled with pine, sage, floral scents, the rush of cold or hot wind in one's face, the sounds of rushing waters, animal cries, the textured touch of sandstone, bark, and grassy meadows, hikers' senses are enlivened, their minds become aware of the body. If the person is willing, an experience with nature clears the mind. Being away from our daily routines means freedom from the demanding roles and expectations these roles entail. In nature we are free from civilization, and are left with ourselves, where the well-spring of our fulfillment originates.

In nature, individuals feel more at home in their own body. The exercise from a strenuous or even moderate hike releases endorphins, chemical mood enhancers which act almost like opiates, enabling the individual to experience a heightened sense of well-being and connection with oneself. As a person feels more connected to the physical self, he or she is better able to experience the emotions and energy present in their body. The person lives a more authentic life.

HIKING ENCOURAGES INDEPENDENCE

In his book *The Road Less Traveled*, M. Scott Peck observed that of the serious debilitating behaviors in the United States, most were comprised of psychiatric dependency disorders. Certain aspects of hiking counter this trend by offering the individual alternative ways to grow independently.

Solitude

The solitude of nature, experienced through hiking, helps unclutter our minds. We are stimulated by the natural world and left with a clearer sense of ourselves. When we become aware of our aloneness, we also become aware of the relationship that we've created with ourselves. Who is this person that I've taken out into the wilderness? What is my attitude toward myself?

The act of being alone on the trail moves us away from the false sense of feeling that what others give us makes us who we are. Solitude helps us to detach from artificial dependencies like creature comforts, being surrounded by friends, or a desk plaque to remind us of who we are in this life and how needed we are. Solitude mirrors to us our inner strength and confidence that we often bury when assuming social roles or reacting to other people's demands and expectations. It is hiking that brings us into the solitude found in nature.

When hikers choose to hike alone, they are forced to become self-reliant. Aloneness on the trail teaches people that they can succeed, finish a task, find the strength and skills within themselves to handle whatever comes along. A sense of self-satisfaction fills people after returning home from their trek. They came, they hiked, they saw, and they enjoyed!

While building independence, solo hiking helps release the individual from dependency. Much of the pain and anxiety attached to dependency comes from the frustration people feel when they are not accepted or loved. It is easy to walk through crowds unnoticed and unwelcomed. On the trail, however, there is no one there to set up the perception of rejection. In nature, solo hikers find freedom from their own need for others that too often goes unanswered. Instead, individuals experience their own self-love and acceptance. With every step, through every beautiful scene, the hiker is reminded that all is well. John Muir once observed that all a person had to do was to "walk away in any direction and taste the freedom of the mountaineer. Climb the mountains and get their good tidings. Nature's peace will flow into you as sunshine flows into trees. The winds will blow their own freshness into you, and the storms their energy, while cares will drop off like autumn leaves."

Time-Out from Society
Being in nature is like a meditation—often we are freed from the complexities and ideas inherited from our culture and left with the simplicity of being ourselves. We instead enjoy a "time out," a clear mind and calm feelings.

Choice and Commitment
Hiking involves making choices. A person chooses to hike a given trail at a given time. No one forces him or her to take to the hills, drive to a trailhead, or begin the journey. Com-

mitment naturally follows choice. Following through on a choice is commitment to oneself to "do the hike," to leave civilization behind and enter the natural world. No journey ever takes place if people wait for something to happen that will magically transport them into the wilderness.

Goethe observed that until one is committed, there is hesitancy which ensures ineffectiveness. However, the moment someone definitely commits, then Providence moves to help that person. Things occur to help that otherwise would not have happened, all directed toward fulfilling the needs and dreams of the person making those commitments. To begin hiking, to choose a lifestyle of hiking several times a month, is to begin creating those occurrences Goethe spoke of.

Planning and Problem Solving
Hiking further enhances personal independence through planning, analysis, and problem solving. If someone wants to walk in a desert, he or she must determine the most comfortable and safest weather conditions for this kind of hike. The individual will often consult weather reports, maps, road conditions, and anything else that will affect the trip.

Planning is required. How much food and drink should I bring? What should I wear and who should I take? Should I take my dog? Some trails do not allow dogs or are unsafe for them. Some human companions are also sometimes best left at home! How long a person will be out, how far they will go, what possible safety concerns exist—these are aspects of a hike that require problem-solving skills.

Mental preparation is about as important as physical preparation. Have a good, positive attitude when you head outdoors. Don't think you will conquer nature. It's not meant to be conquered. It's meant to be enjoyed and cherished. But, of course, hikers must use their best judgment, knowing that any minute nature can take an unexpected turn.

Be mentally prepared for such twists as a change in weather, sliding rocks, or getting lost. Take time before you hike to feel familiar with the wilderness you're going into. Read material about hiking through that area, study maps, and visualize what it will be like once you are there. Go as nature's student and be ready for its teachings. Such planning can take the fear factor out of the proposed hike, but definitely not the excitement!

During the hike, events might take place that demand more problem solving and decision making. Weather conditions could change, accidents might happen, a better, more scenic route might present itself. Hiking is an ongoing process, requiring independent judgment and actions, except when hiking with others, in which case cooperative skills can be drawn upon and enhanced.

Responsibility
The physical, emotional, and personal benefits of any hike are the direct result of the decisions, planning, and analysis that the individual made before and during the hike. Hiking, therefore, links cause to effect. What a person does in the initial phases of a hike affects what kind of experience they will have later. Hiking teaches responsibility in a simple yet sometimes big way.

I once was a co-leader on a 16-mile hike in which the other co-leader raced ahead; I led the group of twenty hikers along a section of the trail I was unfamiliar with. After a few miles, the terrain became a junglelike bushwhack. I needed to find a way to bypass massive boulders blocking the trail. We would have had to stay in the canyon overnight had I not sent two scouts to backtrack and look for a route out. A good trail was discovered and the hike ended at a local restaurant with beer and pizza. I learned some valuable lessons about preparation and logistics that I have never forgotten. This experience helped me grow into a more responsible trail guide and value the worth of proper trip planning.

Many events linked to individual responsibility occur during a hike. If you run out of water on a hot day, fail to pack your rain gear during a storm, or forget your sunscreen on a sunny day, you'll quickly learn that your well-being is really up to you and no one else.

HIKING BUILDS SELF-ESTEEM AND CHARACTER

Any skill learned can be a boost to self-esteem. Any challenge met results in character growth. Hiking facilitates both. A hiker can learn how to read a map and what gear to take. Weather analysis, trip planning, and conditioning are part of the preparation. Finishing a demanding alpine hike up mountain trails or across open desert shows the individual that he or she has the strength and resolve to meet other life challenges. Being alone in nature helps people realize that they are on good terms with themselves; they have enough confidence to be with themselves. The word "confidence" comes from the Latin word that means "to look at oneself, to engage oneself"—exactly what happens to the person who walks through nature.

People have shared with me how the confidence they gained on the trail helped them leave difficult relationships, change jobs, or strike out in new career directions. Goal setting is fulfilled in the accomplishment of a hike, with the many mini-goals of preparation and execution that constitute any hike.

Hiking allows you to go at your own rate, slow down or stop and examine what's around you, and take in the splendor nature offers. In this sense, hiking is an experience that gives control to the hiker. There are few deadlines on the trail. You can turn back at any point, continue on, or linger for hours at any place you choose. Hiking helps a person set priorities, regain control of their own time, and thereby build self-confidence.

Problem solving and crisis management skills learned on the trail further build self-confidence. Hikers sometimes get lost but generally find their way back. Injuries might occur; learning how to treat them so that you can hike in comfort and safety is a confidence builder. Many skills and interests learned while hiking become foundation skills that can be built upon, often directed toward other outdoor pursuits such as mountaineering, river rafting, canoeing, rock climbing, or backpacking.

The reward is instantaneous self-confidence. A person doesn't have to wait a month to reap the benefits of a hike well done. In this same vein, hiking gives the immediate satisfaction of closure. Every hike has a beginning, a middle, and an end, and when you reach the trail's finish, you feel a sense of completeness. What you learn and enjoy on the trail you keep.

Hiking isn't contrived. What you see, you internalize; what you do is yours forever. Because it is kinetic body movement through nature, and simple in itself, it simplifies the psyche of the hiker. It isn't complicated and doesn't require a great deal of skill, but it does require preparation. Hiking takes you into nature's purity, open spaces, and unconditional presence. It encourages our own honesty. No politics, no opinion polls, just the individual and the surrounding, soothing envelope of nature.

Hiking in the openness of the west often fills you with a sense of endless possibility. Horizons stretch to infinity, and being able to see for miles often leaves one with a feeling of safety. This expansiveness can facilitate hikers feeling open to themselves, to their feelings, to their life and its direction, and to humanity.

People have shared with me how hiking has helped reduce or even erase certain fears they may have had before they began hiking. Many thought dayhiking to be the same as rock climbing, backpacking, or mountaineering. It is none of these, and when novices discover this, they immediately feel relieved. Ironically, many hikers expand their outdoor interests to include these more demanding skill sports. With every hike, their confidence with themselves and with being outdoors grows. A person begins to know nature, its seasons, personality, and habits. Nature and the outdoors become familiar friends, comfortable to be with. Being alone soon loses its fear factor. The hiker discovers that the person he or she takes into nature is more confident, more aware, and more alive than ever before.

The elements of confidence, responsibility, character building, decision making, and independence that hiking facilitates in the individual are known and documented from such outdoor programs as Outward Bound and scouting. People value and need activities that, when committed to and completed, give them real and enduring growth of character and nourishment of soul. Hiking does this.

HIKING ENHANCES SELF-AWARENESS

As a person successfully clears the mind from the concerns and distractions of daily life, the individual is in closer contact with themselves. Personal feelings, attitudes, goals, and hopes, sometimes buried or of a lower priority than daily demands of job and family, begin to surface. People are often surprised during a hike to discover some meaningful aspect of their own destiny, perhaps a new career direction or a creative outlet. The individual is free from judgments, comparisons, and expectations. Nature accepts each visitor unconditionally.

On a hike, the individual can more easily tap into their own aspirations and dreams. When the demands of society fade, we are left with ourselves. Emotional baggage drops away with each step taken into the wilderness or the gentle recesses of nature. Quiet pools, lakes, meadows, plateaus and mountain vistas, or desert expanses offer hikers freedom from their own cluttered minds. Nature is friendly.

Hiking encourages the individual to become more aware of his or her surroundings, to see where he or she is going. Hiking helps us acknowledge that we live in a much larger world than our own concerns and roles. This results in us gaining valuable perspectives into our own lives.

HIKING FACILITATES LIFE CHANGES

Few people ever go through life without making major changes. These life changes often include choice of career, where to live, choosing a life partner, and whether to raise a family. Each one of these and other life conditions represents a system, or paradigm, whose psychological environment is colored by our values and attitudes, needs, desires, perceptions, beliefs, and expectations.

Whenever someone changes a job, for instance, that person quickly sees what the real dynamics were in their particular workplace. The conflicts the individual might have had with the "company culture" interfering with their personal values and needs becomes painfully clear. The person might have needed more freedom to be creative, solve problems, and participate more in the decision making process, while the corporate culture and the boss prevented their acting in this more independent style.

We move through our daily life within these paradigms, such as career and relationships, our needs sometimes met, sometimes not. Over time there can arise a sense of frustration and unfulfillment. Perhaps our career has exhausted us; it no longer is a vehicle of personal growth and satisfaction. We feel that something is missing. This dissatisfaction prompts us to examine our jobs or careers and find where positive changes might be made, some new aspects or responsibilities added, and others discarded. We are in the midst of making a paradigm shift, a life change. Just like the individual who changes careers, we need to find our niche that allows us to best express and be who we are.

Many people experience pressure to make life changes in their personal relationships and marriages. Needs are no longer being met, values change, friendship wanes. We stop choosing to satisfy our mates or they stop caring for us. We begin drifting away from the relationship and experience the gnawing pressure and anxiety of making a change.

Or we might feel that the area we live in is no longer interesting or that we've taken advantage of all that it has to offer. We've been there, done that—to the point of exhaustion. These, and so many other life changes or pressures to change, represent the process of making a paradigm shift in some aspect of our lives. And we find that the longer we stay put and do nothing, the more frustrated and unhappy we feel. People or situations that enter our lives, new tools we discover or that present themselves to us, are welcome because they facilitate this process of change. Hiking is one of these effective "tools" that help us make successful and satisfying life changes.

The Nature of a Paradigm Shift
Paradigms and life situations are challenged when we feel the need for change because some of our needs not being met. We begin affecting life change as we grow in awareness of and identify those things in our life that do not "fit," that remain unfulfilled. How can hiking help us make this change? Hiking through nature is a perfect setting for leaving our paradigm or life situation behind for just long enough, and with the right conditions, that we begin to feel and see what concerns us. By creating physical distance between, for example, the workplace and ourselves, we create the detachment helpful in acknowledging what it is that bothers us. We create a space in which to evaluate a challenging part of our lives, assessing what can be done to get us where we want to be.

Many hikers experience a kind of decompression and release when taking to nature and leaving behind daily life. Being away from a given life situation encourages us to see it for what it is, to honestly take responsibility for the part we have played in creating our dissatisfaction, and to take responsibility for choices that will lead us into a more fulfilling life situation.

Hiking through forests, over hills, and up mountains brings us into vital contact with nature's physical reality, scents, temperatures, wetness, dryness, colors, etc. Nature is nonjudgmental—safe. Out in the wilderness no one finds fault with the change process that we are going through. On the trail, inspiration comes easier, as we get in touch with our deeper selves. While hiking, we can free ourselves from too closely identifying with a given situation that we need to change. We gain a clarifying perspective from which to make decisions that will alter our lives in a way that will satisfy us.

Many times during a hike I have heard someone cry out "aha" as some meaningful idea or inspiration came to that person. Hiking was the vehicle that awakened these insights. We are given a new vision of what we want our future to be.

A friend once visited me in Colorado during a time when he was contemplating making a major career change. During his stay, we dayhiked, often discussing the process of change that he was experiencing. After evaluating his experiences while hiking, he noticed that he was better able to clarify the issues involved. We were able to identify the following connection between hiking and making life changes.

Any life change includes the interaction between our self (or self-image), what we are aware of (our conscious mind), and what lies beyond our awareness (our subconscious mind). Hiking energizes us, helping us make the first step in any change: becoming more willing and open to making changes. In feeling the beautiful tranquillity in nature and gaining additional self-confidence through hiking, we grow from an attitude of just "accepting" change to actually "wanting" it.

Hiking does many things that encourage positive self-image and personal enhancement. We accomplish our goal of doing the hike, often alone in our solitude, having prepared well while testing our physical and psychological powers to successfully complete the hike. We have become a "doer," which in turn has added to our sense of self—more confident, assured, grounded in our own mind and body, energized, at peace.

Our conscious mind has been altered by the great power of being in nature, along with the release of negative ideas and self-defeating attitudes or images about ourselves. Instead, we picture ourselves as "outdoor skilled," capable of journeying through wilderness, for many miles of often uphill climbs, seeing beautiful scenes that help replace any negative "life memories and images" we may have brought into nature.

Our very subconscious has also been changed for the better with the subtle messages we give ourselves during every hike: "I came into the land, made friends with it and with myself, drew strength from its healing spiritual powers, found strength and confidence within myself, affirming my own goodness and power, having surrendered all fear— I am alive! I am myself! I can and will achieve!"

Now we are closer to harmony and balance. Our conscious self, subconscious self, and self-image have been positively realigned and enhanced through hiking. We are in a much better condition of wellness for making successful life changes and achieving goals.

I believe that nature encourages optimism by its composite of beauty and pleasing physical/sensual environment.

Great and expansive vistas open us up to our own possibilities. The same power that fashioned the soaring mountains, the raging rivers, the quiet flower-filled meadow, and life-giving green forests seems to energize the hiker with every step. Indeed, the energy we receive from the exercise of hiking and the soothing effects of nature encourages us to focus on our concerns, commit to change with our newfound rejuvenation, and face the challenges with hope and faith. We have taken the risk of hiking the wilderness; nature now encourages us to take the necessary risks to empty our lives of what we don't want and fill them with what we do value and need.

Too often the pressure of needing to make changes and the anticipation of how those changes might affect us drain us of the very energy we need to deal with our issues. We often feel listless and even depressed. Hiking restores that energy to us while countering those negative influences.

Along the trail, with our minds now more at ease and quieted, we have the opportunity to evaluate the steps we need to take to positively effect change in our lives. Perhaps we need to pull away from certain nonsupportive people who have held us back. Or we might acknowledge our need to bring into our lives positive people who share our values and vision. Whatever we choose to do, the space in our hearts and minds that hiking expands will offer us the setting to realize the changes we need to make.

Besides shedding unwanted individuals, we most often need to abandon ideas, assumptions, attitudes, perceptions, and values that no longer work for us. Nature affords us a place to deliberately examine all these mental constructs which impact and guide our lives. What have we outgrown? What has proven false? What simply no longer works? I have found that looking into my mind during a hike is like a walking meditation. Somehow the fear element is extracted from our mind-sets while we are in nature. By drawing closer to our more confident selves, we become less dominated by our negative emotions and thoughts.

Hiking increases our confidence in many ways. The fact that we've taken ourselves into the wild to self-examine our lives shows us just how strong we really are. We have dared to face ourselves. And by mastering the skills needed for hiking, we have a basis to qualify ourselves as an accomplished individual in that particular area. For some people, that confidence is just what they need to transfer a sense of well-being and can-do attitude to the life challenges facing them.

Hiking helps some people move from being overly mental to connecting with their physical, active self. Real change requires doing rather than thinking. A person cannot simply contemplate making changes, fantasizing or hoping for things to be different. Yet there are individuals who find it very difficult to implement decisions with actions. If these people can use hiking to move into an energized action mode, then they can also begin making those decisions that eventually effect change.

NATURE MIRRORS THE PSYCHE

Nature provides the soul with rich images that reflect the condition of the human psyche and lessons helpful for daily living. Storms gather in nature just as conflicts rise in any person's life. But they eventually pass, as do our life trials and tribulations. Quiet meadows mirror the quiet recesses of the human heart that must take stock of itself and weigh its aspirations and dreams. Nature provides us with a thousand changing moods: cloud formations, sunlight that suggests moments of inspiration or periods of withdrawn gestation, the arrangement of plant life that hints of our own ordered or chaotic inner world. Nature, then, becomes a teacher to us, reminding visitors of the simple truths they often miss during the hurry and dash of daily living.

During a hike it is sometimes a rewarding exercise to leave the trail and sit quietly atop a rock overlook, beside a running stream, or in a quiet wood or meadow. Empty your mind of everything and just see what is around you. Let the scene speak to you, inspiring its own insights and drawing from your own soul and heart their deeper truths.

Lessons abound in nature. Shortly into a hike, the great truth in life emerges: there is no turning back, just the invitation to go forward. During a hike, gauge a far distance and surprise yourself with how quickly you reach it if you are persistent and continue your stride. And with every mountain we struggle up, we enjoy the downward slope and flatlands that life also offers to anyone who mistakenly believes that only steep upslopes are their fate.

HIKING CREATES A NATURAL AND POSITIVE IDENTITY

Ask most people about their lives, and they will begin with stories that include problems, failures, and conflicts. Even when we are alone and reflecting on what it means to "be me," we tend to accent the negative. People beat themselves up with painful memories and grudges they keep.

Hiking during the many changes of the four seasons, alone or with friends, helps to erase these negative memories and identities. If people can enjoy nature on a weekly basis, or at least several times a month, they soon find that each hike becomes a powerfully positive experience, an enjoyable memory that they remember often to taste its rewarding pleasures—such as inspiring scenes, closeness with others, exhilarating energy, and enhanced confidence. Their identity now becomes "this person who enjoyed these beautiful trails with good friends or worthy companions (including your dog!), and experienced many hours of enriching, enjoyable natural contact."

I have hiked several times a week during the last ten years. My perspective has continually changed for the better. Instead of being reminded of stressful situations from daily living, I think of countless refreshing hikes through colorful deserts, across plateaus and mesas, into wild, alpine-forested mountains or canyons, over soft-flowing prairie grasses, alongside still and peaceful blue lakes and pristine rivers, and under brilliant topaz skies. I have grown close to the natural treasures that I have allowed into my soul. With every visit into the world of nature, I am now reminded of a previous uplifting hiking experience.

Being out in sunshine has an additional benefit. Lack of sufficient light has been shown to bring on depression. Sunshine generates positive feelings and optimism. Hiking memories are easily associated with the "up" moods created by sun and blue skies.

HIKING CREATES A SENSE OF HOME

More than 20 percent of all Americans move every two years. This up-and-out-of-here trend generates a declining sense of home. People feel less comfortable where they live. There is a declining sense of community, of belonging, as our physical and social surroundings become less familiar. Hiking counters this trend.

N. Scott Momaday in his book *The Way to Rainy Mountain* writes that "Once in his life a man ought to concentrate his mind upon the remembered earth, I believe. He ought to give himself up to a particular landscape in his experience, to look at it from as many angles as he can, to wonder about it, to dwell upon it. He ought to imagine that he touches it with his hands at every season and listens to the sounds that are made upon it. He ought to recollect the glare of the noon and all the colors of the dawn and dusk." Momaday asserts here the necessity for a human being to "know" and to "experience" the land that surrounds him or her, to partake of a physical and sensual communion with what resides in and on the land and the forces of nature that sweep that land and make their presence felt through the seasons—thereby unlocking the spirit of that place.

In so doing, a person makes him or herself at home and establishes an almost mystic connection with where he or she lives. To thus "know" the land is to be really "home" where one lives, in the fullest sense, with the same nature that defines one's daily experience—the shape and color of the mountains, the change of the trees and the grasses, the look of the land from all the various perspectives it can be seen from, even to the sweep of the horizons and how the clouds pass through the sky, the different feel of rain and sun on the skin, what fragrances the winds carry, and how sunlight changes each portrait that nature paints at each hour of the day. What is familiar encourages a sense of home.

Over a ten-year period I have hiked almost every trail within 75 miles of where I live in Southern California. Whenever I look up to the surrounding mountains, peer into nearby canyons or across open desert, a sense of home and belonging well up within me. I have visited every peak, scoured every canyon. I know intimately, as only a hiker can know, what the physical world around me consists of.

What a contrast, this stability of mountains and canyons, forest and trail, with the changing scene of streets, neighborhoods, and neighbors. I walk hallowed, familiar good ground. I have become friends with the desert, the mountains that fill my horizons, and vast arrays of plant and animal life, having seen coyote, golden eagles, red-tailed hawks, countless varieties of cactus, red and purple carpets of verbena, and the purple mountain lupine after bountiful winter rains. I have known cooling, down-canyon breezes on a warm spring day, tasted the heavy scent of purple sage atop high desert mountain slopes, and witnessed the full moon rise over wild, twisted, and uplifted canyonlands.

Anyone living anywhere in America can experience nature, either in or near their neighborhoods or within a few hours' drive, and learn to be at home where they live. Strike up a relationship with nature and learn something about who you are. We are at home wherever we allow the earth to reach out and touch us, reminding us once again of a friendship that never ends and that is always there to partake of.

HIKING HELPS US BE CHILDLIKE AGAIN

One of my favorite treks to take visitors or new hikers on is a hike through an uplifted desert, canyon, and mountain area near Palm Springs, California, known as Painted Canyon. This region is a mixture of twisted rock, narrow canyons, and colorful soil and rock formations. On this hike, hikers are particularly excited when they reach the area known as Ladder Canyon. Each person must climb up a series of ladders and negotiate through winding, narrow passageways that allow them to touch both walls of the canyon simultaneously. This trip turns adults into wide-eyed ten-year-olds as they scramble over, through, and around exotic geological formations. A sense of wonder, surprise, and excitement fills the air. People laugh easily, extend a helping hand to fellow hikers, and generally forget the responsibilities and reserved behavior of adulthood.

Most hikes allow people to rediscover the little kid within. Stunning floral displays of purple lupine, red Indian paintbrush, blue asters, and wild rose in mountain meadows; expansive vistas from mountain or plateau trails; the serenity of grazing deer; the unexpected appearance of a bighorn sheep or the stately flight of an eagle or hawk—all inspire our childlike sense of wonder and awe at nature's elegance. We become explorers, like Lewis and Clark, Powell, or Fremont, from the age of discovery. For if this is our first time seeing the Grand Canyon, hiking the Narrows of Zion National Park, tramping backcountry Rocky

Mountain trails, viewing the wide expanses of Canyonlands or the Appalachian Mountains, are we not witnessing with the same thrill the powerful newness that nature provides first-time visitors, whether 200 years ago or just yesterday?

With every hike I become a kid again. My tempered and experienced adult self becomes the willing servant of my child self that seeks to see, touch, feel, and wonder in the freedom and openness that hiking into nature offers. In the backcountry, along pine- and flower-scented forest paths—I am reborn again.

HIKING KEEPS US IN THE PRESENT MOMENT

The psychology of meditation teaches that our awareness of the past often brings guilt, while our preoccupation with the future can create fear and anxiety about expectations. One of the secrets of wholeness is to remain in the dynamic present, involved with whatever action is currently taking place.

Hiking is an experience that encourages the individual to remain in the present moment. The loveliness of the scenery constantly draws the hiker into his or her surroundings. Trail conditions require the person to pay attention to each step. Cares and demands of daily life are left behind. Hikers are instead offered the tranquillity of the present moment in the stillness of natural surroundings.

Often during a hike, people fixate on some especially serene and majestic sight, or lose themselves in the changing exuberance of passing cloud formations. In every instance, the person is drawn back into the present moment, back into the wholeness of his or her own self. In nature, what we see replaces what we think. We become one with all creation. In the "doing" of a hike, we find the clarity of our being. Hiking becomes a meditation, sometimes in motion and at other times completely still and silent.

HIKING SHOWS US THE GIFT OF SELF-LOVE

Who has given any hiker all the good, the joy, the fun, and the healing that he or she experiences on any hike? Nature sets the table and invites us to the banquet, but it's the individual who accepts that invitation by stepping forth on the trail. The joy of hiking is a cooperative venture between ourselves and the natural world. We learn with every step we take, with every exhilarating moment along the trail, that it is we who have esteemed ourselves enough to treat ourselves to the hike, to love both the journey and the journeyer.

Hiking is an exercise in self-love. We reach for the best that nature has to offer. Our joy becomes appreciation, then transforms itself into gratitude. Out of gratitude, we tell others of the goodness of our experiences, inviting them to become hikers, too, and discover for themselves the many rewards of this enriching pastime. Along the trail we find that nature has made us equal. We are all on the trail of life, and each person becomes a potential traveling companion, no matter how brief the encounter.

Hiking has much to offer anyone. But it is never hiking itself or any specific hike that ultimately holds the key for enhanced well-being. Hiking is a particularly good means to this worthy end. Still, it remains up to each individual to create his or her own experience from the rich materials nature provides.

STRESS MANAGEMENT AND HIKING

Great Escapes
Into Serenity

"Survival studies have shown that those who adapt success-
fully in a stress situation . . . possess determination, a positive
degree of stubbornness, well-defined values, self-direction,
and a belief in the goodness of mankind. [They are] also
cooperative. [They are] also kind to [themselves]. [They do]
not fear pain or discomfort, nor [do they] seek to punish
[themselves] with them. [They are] not . . . self-hater[s]."

—*Larry Dean Olsen,* Outdoor Survival Skills *(1973)*

The process of stress management begins when individuals acknowledge that they are bothered by stress
overload or exhaustion. They can then define the problem,
the sources, or the causes, formulating various descriptions
of how they see stress being created and its effects on their
lives. If they have done this process before, they can remember what strategies they used in the past that worked, and
see if they can apply them to current situations.

Once the various aspects of stress are identified, the focus of stress management returns to the individual: What are their feelings and attitudes about the problem and their ability to cope with their stress? Do they possess the necessary self-love to take specific action to change the stress levels in their life? What are their resources, strengths, support people, someone they can get helpful feedback from? What outcomes do they want to see as a result of their actions? What do they want to change and how do they propose doing it?

During my fifteen years conducting stress management seminars, I have received feedback from hundreds of individuals about what caused their stress and what successful steps they took both to prevent and to release that stress. During this same time I've hiked thousands of miles and have evaluated the relationship between hiking and successful stress management. One truth has become consistently clear to me: Hiking creates a powerful setting for dealing with stress while facilitating effective, immediate stress release.

RELEASE FROM STRESSFUL ENVIRONMENTS

First, hiking addresses the environmental factors that contribute to high stress levels. Population and crowds, job pressures, deadlines, excessive noise, enclosed buildings, pavement, advertisement ploys, being in crowds but not feeling "connected," and dealing with certain types of individuals are all environmental stress factors. On the trail, out in nature, none of these environmental stressors exist. The very act of leaving this type of environment creates a positive, stress-free setting in which individuals can recuperate as well as address the causes of their stress.

It has been long known that human beings have a definite physical requirement for maintaining a healthy distance between each other. We need our "space." The high population density of cities contributes to the creation of stress due to the crowded feelings generated in city living—"loss of space." Parks have always offered some relief for this stress from overcrowding, but nothing helps this condition more than simply being in the great outdoors, hiking some open-vista trail where few if any people are encountered during the hike.

Hikers experience instant relief the moment they set foot on the trail and view peaceful, majestic mountains, prairie, desert sands, lakes, forests, etc. Throughout a hike, other stress management processes begin to assert themselves.

RELEASE FROM PHYSICAL STRESS

The consistent exercise afforded by hiking, combined with fresh air, scenic and relaxed natural settings, and freedom from stress sources, together with the company of an enjoyable hiking companion (human or canine), all make hiking a powerful tool in any successful stress management program. And these benefits are just from the physical components of hiking.

Muscle Tension
Ask any massage therapist why people feel good after a massage; they will tell you that stress is retained in the muscles of

the body, and that massage releases the tension stored in those muscles. Tight muscles constrict blood flow, which reduces the blood's ability to carry away the waste products, such as lactic acid, of stress and muscle activity.

Lisa, a massage therapist from Boulder, Colorado, and an avid hiker, has observed that stress produces physiological and psychological changes that affect a person's well-being, productivity, and personality. Stress reactions include increased blood pressure, shallow breathing, adrenaline production, and increased flow of blood to the extremities. All these are symptoms of the "fight or flight" response. Stress is often a response to a perceived threat. In a state of stress, blood flow to the brain is decreased, thwarting one's ability to think clearly.

You can reduce this stress response and increase blood flow to the muscles by stretching them, breathing deeply, drinking plenty of water, and receiving massage therapy. The person receiving the massage feels relaxed, their muscles softened, no longer in hard knots. With this muscle release comes stress release. At best, however, massage is only a temporary fix.

Hiking acts as nature's massage; the exercise from walking, climbing, stretching over obstacles on the trail, and sweating all combine to release muscle tension just like a regular massage does. The cardiovascular workout that hiking achieves increases blood flow, which helps flush toxins out of the body. As the hiker relaxes during a hike, energy is released into the body. The hiker feels energized and more confident, and this helps the individual to more successfully deal with stress.

Hiking increases circulation and deepens breathing, thus reversing the effects of stress. Hikers say they feel better physically and mentally after a hike. "The physicaɪ ᴸ efits I get from hiking are incredible," says hiker Wanda Nesté of Palm Springs, California. "But [it's] not just physical, it's a stress relief. It clears your mind and gives you a peaceful feeling." Hiking is a stress reliever.

High Blood Pressure
Researchers from the University of Western Ontario recently discovered that stress is a more potent contributor to heart attacks and strokes than smoking or diabetes. Exercise was suggested as a way of reducing stress and thereby reducing the chances of suffering from heart attacks and strokes. In other words, to lower high blood pressure and reduce the stress level, one could hike.

After a weekend of hiking I often get my blood pressure taken. It is consistently lower than when I am not hiking, and over many months, my blood pressure drifts downward as a result of weekly hiking. These changes, along with the calming influence offered by nature's serenity, enable the individual to have heightened clarity of thought. This gives the person a new vantage point from which to view their reality and more effectively deal with the mental causes of stress as well as lessening the confusion stress often induces.

Hiking also contributes to a lessening of stress from pathological-medical stressors. Many seniors from the retirement resort area of Palm Springs, California, have validated the amazing effects of hiking on their coronary and hypertension conditions. Those who weekly hike over 15 miles (many are good for 25-plus) cite weight loss, lower blood pressure (I've known many instances where blood pressures came down from the 140/110 area to 120/80 after several months or even weeks of regular hiking), improved dietary practices, and even a noticeable improvement in heart conditions.

Substance Abuse

Trails are usually free from the self-imposed stressors of tobacco (in all my years of hiking, I've seen only one person smoke on the trail), sugar and fat, substance abuse, and sluggishness caused by a sedentary lifestyle.

Sleep Loss

I cannot emphasize enough that lack of exercise is often the cause of poor sleeping habits. Hiking offers a refreshing form of exercise so necessary for healthy sleeping patterns. After a hike, the individual is treated to a restful, full night's sleep, which relieves stress caused by sleep loss, thereby continuing the helpful benefits from hiking.

Depression

Chronic anxiety and depression also lessen when you hike. Much repressed anger, often the cause of depression, is stored in the muscles but is successfully released during moderate to strenuous hikes.

MOTIVATION

During my stress management seminars, I ask participants to imagine themselves walking through a parking lot and suddenly stepping on a nail that penetrates their foot. What would their reaction be? Pain, of course. What would they do once they felt that pain? Pull the nail out and go see a doctor immediately. Could anyone imagine somebody continuing to walk with the nail still penetrating their foot, forcing it more deeply and painfully inward? No, of course not.

Then I ask if anyone has ever experienced an ongoing, painful emotion and stress situation. Yes, most of us have. But we continued to live with those uncomfortable emotions and stress, perhaps creating even more painful emotions. Isn't this akin to walking with a nail in our foot? Why don't we take those "stress and painful emotion nails" out of our lives and our psyches? Sometimes we lack the motivation to do so, the perspective and honesty to face what is going on, and sometimes knowledge and skill. Stress management and reduction begins with the proper motivation to deal with stress. No amount of knowledge about what causes stress will work if it is not accompanied by motivation to apply that knowledge.

It takes energy to take the necessary steps beforehand to prepare for a hike and drive to the trailhead. These acts of preparation and follow-through can be summed up as a simple act of self-love, the individual acting on behalf of their own best interests and needs. The total feel-good results after a hike reinforce the perception in hikers that they have done something good for themselves. This love of self constitutes the motivation for further dealing with one's stress. People who loathe themselves fail to care for their own needs, but a hiker has already started in motion the additional energy necessary to deal with and reduce their stress levels.

PERSPECTIVE

Most people find, at certain times of their life, a need to take "time out" from all the pressures, demands, or exhausted living and job patterns. Often after changing jobs, moving to another part of the country, or leaving a relationship, we need to catch our breath, assess, evaluate, and reprioritize our lives. During a hike, individuals withdraw mentally (and, of course, physically) from the sources of their stress. As they do so, they gain a clarity of thought and perspective. In the backcountry, away from the judgment of others, it becomes easier to both monitor our life and acknowledge the existence of our personal stress and our stress-producing lifestyles.

A hike is a kind of "moving meditation," a chance to see what is going on in one's life and begin taking steps to detach from the causes. Being in nature supports the perspective of discriminating between "what I am doing to create my own stress" and "the role others play in adding to my stress levels," between "what I can and cannot control." In nature we don't have to play games, defend ourselves against the boss or someone else's manipulations, in order to avoid more stress by incurring someone's anger or jealousy. Life problems and stressors are given a perspective that often escapes the individual when they are back in the world, totally plugged in to the demands and roles that create their stress.

The benefit of perspective frequently begins with the experience of open spaces that hiking trails often bring the hiker into. The sky opens up to the horizons, the clouds seem to stretch on endlessly, and the sense of expansiveness encourages hikers to honestly reflect on issues related to their own stress.

A member from my hiking club lived in a city more than 100 miles from where we hiked. He was struggling with a painful and involved divorce, but drove every weekend to join us on a hike. In his words, "I was a walking basket case. My financial condition was in ruins, my health was deteriorating, I couldn't sleep well—in short I was at my breaking point and completely stressed out. But those hikes I took on the weekends saved me. I really felt a vast improvement regarding my stress levels, and was able to eventually weather the storm and get my life back in order. While on the trail, I could see things that I always overlooked or missed completely when back in the city. I attribute my improved condition to the benefits given me from hiking."

RESPONDING TO SPECIFIC STRESSORS

By gaining perspective during a hike, the individual becomes aware of very specific sources of stress. All the distractions of job and lifestyle momentarily disappear. Those who have the necessary motivation and perspective to respond to their stress begin formulating choices and specific actions designed to deal with and prevent that stress. How does hiking become a part of these solutions?

Negative Ideas and Emotions

Many stress experiences result from people reacting to negative, stress-producing ideas such as "I may lose my job," "This person I care about may not welcome my suggestion," "I might be called upon to speak in front of a group," etc. Negative, fear-ladened ideas are often the trigger for a person creating a stressful response to those ideas.

Hiking helps release the stress from negative ideas by requiring people to focus on the immediate here-and-now. Hikers have to see where they are going, where to step, and what is around them. This attention to the present moment and its demands lessens the creation and flow of fear-producing ideas. While hiking, people feel good, enjoy the beauty of nature, are physically drawn to sights, smells, textures, tastes, and sounds—bird and animal life, pine, sage, wildflowers, textured sandstone, and exquisite rock formations. They are too busy enjoying their hike to let negative ideas produce negative emotions. Hiking helps calm the overactive mind, lessens the flow of negative ideas, and actually helps the individual detach from those very ideas, roles, or self-imposed expectations that often create stress.

Something very powerful happens during a hike. The incessant flow of unwanted ideas or concepts, often times negative stress-producers, lessens or even stops entirely. The hiker experiences the health of the calm, empty mind. Even the experience of ideas as being more "real" than they are or more real to us than warranted is lessened. Persons, "hikers," experience their own well-being and wholeness—they see themselves as the creator and user of ideas rather than the victim of concepts allowed to dominate and direct their lives.

Negative feelings, like negative thoughts, often create stress. Hiking helps reduce a person's stress by releasing the grip of negative emotions. Many people find hiking a kind of play time, where a sense of discovery and adventure, coupled with freedom from urban responsibilities and the newness of trails not yet visited, conjures up a happy, childlike identity. Exhilaration, anticipation of what lies around the corner, the majestic presence of mountains, valley vistas, quiet lake or meadow settings, and countless similar scenic encounters along the way create enriching, uplifting emotions. The child within is alive and well in the heart of any hiker on such trails. Even the sunshine and blue skies combat the stress from depressive feelings. Nature heals with colors, be it the pink and red sunsets-in-sandstone of Utah, Arizona, and New Mexico, the rich, quieting, yet vibrant greens of the forests, or the bold relief of swirling white clouds in a western sky caressing stately purple, gray, and red mountains.

Negative emotions are pushed aside by the easy sharing that happens on the trail between friends and strangers alike. Experienced hikers know better than to introduce competitive stress or one-upmanship on the trail. Instead, hiking often brings out the best in people, a feeling of comradeship in nature where no one is a threat. Meaningful communication produces positive feelings between people, leaving little room for negative emotions.

Self-Absorption

Perhaps it's the powerful, direct, sense-stimulated experience of nature and the aesthetic enjoyment nature offers us that cause the overactive mind to relax and free the individual from the tyranny of conceptual addiction. Whatever the root causes, hiking involves people in a positive experience other than their own problems, thereby freeing them from the stress of excessive self-absorption.

Mind-Body Imbalance

Hiking facilitates the integration of mind, body, self, and nature, grounding us in the very act of walking on the earth. This experience of oneness and wholeness further lessens the stress that individuals bring with them to the trail. Feeling more rooted in positive, uplifting experiences, hikers freely release many of the negative ideas they once were obsessed about. Being more in touch with one's loving and confident self naturally releases unwanted stress—the positive and the negative cannot occupy the same psychic space at the same time.

Much of what passes for stress is actually this imbalance between mind and body, a separation of the two that allows negative thoughts to seem more real than warranted. We do make mountains out of molehills, but hiking helps *restore the balance,* thereby reducing stress. Anyone returning from a strenuous 10-mile hike will attest to this powerful experience of feeling more physically and mentally connected to oneself, to heightened energy levels, positive feelings, and a more relaxed, harmonious state of mind and body.

I've known many professional people who worked too long, too hard, neglecting their physical and exercise needs and the strengthening of their body. Once they took up hiking, they were very satisfied with their newfound energy and sense of harmony between their worldly involvements and their recreational needs. Stress management is sometimes no more than reestablishing this balance in our lives.

Fear of the Unknown

Much of what passes as stress is no more than people's fear of the unknown and being out of touch with their own inner strength. Hikers experience their freedom and ability to be away from the crutches and familiarity of civilization when they climb mountain slopes challenging their physical endurance, hike long distances into the wilderness, and feel the serenity of those far-away places rather than their threat. They discover the oneness of all living things, while feeling their personal power from having stepped into and through previously unknown places. Upon returning from a trek into those wild lands, they experience strength from the solitude found in those places.

Feeling Out of Control
The stress that comes from feeling out of control from the pressures and demands of modern living disappear along the trail. Hikers travel where they choose, at their chosen pace, taking time to explore meadows, rivers, mountains or valleys, forests, and plant life without the gnawing interruption of deadlines or artificial constraints. Each hike is a constant chain of personal decisions to examine, look at, feel, and admire various aspects of nature along the way. This is self-empowerment, making choices to do good unto oneself, to act on one's own behalf, on our time, not someone else's.

As powerful as nature is, it also bestows on its visitors the power within themselves, unlocked by the efforts the journey took to worship, in silent awe, the divine presence found throughout nature. What every hiker is offered is the opportunity to take back to the modern world and their hurried lifestyle a greater and deeper experience of themselves and their own worthiness.

Overdependence
Individuals who tend to be too dependent create stress by needing others, always looking for validation from some-

one and something else, and never being completely secure about getting this "fix" from the outside. Hiking encourages independence by forcing individuals to look after themselves in packing gear, food, planning a destination, reading a map, actually arriving at the trail, and completing its many miles. If they hike alone, they feel the additional confidence that comes from facing the wilderness by themselves.

People have shared with me that the simple acts of negotiating rocky terrain, crossing streams, climbing past exposed trail sections, finding directions to a given location, achieving greater elevation gains than ever attempted, and countless other basic tasks one does during a hike all resulted in higher levels of confidence in themselves and in their physical body, its ability to overcome obstacles. Independence is one of the core lessons learned by hiking.

A friend remarks, "I am in my mid-sixties, and took up hiking late in life. Every day for years I would look up to the top of San Jacinto Peak, soaring almost 11,000 feet above where I lived. Once I became a hiker and got in good condition, I knew what I wanted to do: take on that mountain. I finally completed the 'Cactus-to-Clouds' adventure, all 22 miles and 10,500 feet elevation gain in one day. And after that I knew I could do anything."

Self-Will
Ironically, hiking also offers stress management strategies for the individual who pushes their will to the limit, the self-will addict. The physical world is a world of limits. The vast majority of individuals exhaust themselves at some point by climbing to a certain height, traveling a certain distance, enduring particular weather conditions.

Nature seems to say to most of us that it's all right to meet and accept one's limits, it's okay to exhaust oneself. The people who learn this lesson from hiking often return with a greater respect for honoring boundaries that establish balance in their lives. Instead of pushing themselves and others beyond healthy limits, they learn to ease up.

Frustration
Another source of stress for individuals is the frustration of needs, real or perceived. Perhaps they have created expectations too high for themselves or others. On the trail, these excesses are often revealed by the perspective hiking gives us of our beliefs, attitudes, values, etc.; it remains up to individuals to make their expectations conform to a reality that works for instead of against who they really are.

Loneliness
In our modern world, loneliness is a major source of stress. The need to be loved and to love, to feel connected and belonging to and with others, often goes unmet. But in nature there are few people to remind us of what we think we need from them. Nature encourages people to look inward and discover their own goodness and the love they can consistently offer themselves, instead of waiting for it from someone else. It's not that we don't need love, but the oppressive awareness of being unloved is replaced by the recognition of the love that is found both within ourselves and in the very natural world to which hiking brings us. The gifts of nature—color, scents, vistas, scenery, a cooling breeze—are offered freely, unconditionally. After a hike, an aware person knows that they've just been loved. Nature is a very positive place where all the benefits we

receive from having visited the outdoors can be seen as an act of love we have bestowed upon ourselves.

Release from the Stress of Uselessness
Every so often we need to recognize the meaning and purpose of our existence. A life aimlessly lived, without value to the individual and other people, becomes filled with the stress of uselessness. Hiking will not give us our life's purpose, but it does provide a setting in which it might be discovered. Nature, as we've seen in this chapter, offers us freedom from distraction, a quiet place to listen to our own inner stirrings, to hearken to the wellspring of our own souls and hearts.

History is filled with examples of people who have gone to the wilderness in order to find inspiration and direction. Christ visited the wilderness to pray and find direction; Moses went up to Mount Sinai to receive his calling to lead his people out of Egypt; Beethoven retreated to the countryside around Vienna to find the strength to overcome his deafness and release creative energies which helped produce his magnificent symphonies.

On the trail people have shared with me their own search for purpose and healing. After an emotionally painful divorce, a friend traveled to the Canadian Rockies to draw inspiration, heal, and find new meaning for her life. My American Indian friends relate stories of their going out into nature for the purpose of finding their spirit guides, a process known as a "vision quest." Making the trek into the comforting embrace of the land and open sky becomes symbolic of our journey inward. In nature we discover and rediscover who we are, what significance and purpose the challenges, crises, and opportunities of life mean for each of us.

Without this discovery, we live from day to day, existing, struggling, but failing to focus our lives in ways that are touched by love or service. Several years ago I journeyed to Zion National Park in Utah for the purpose of rediscovering more of my own life purpose. I was healing from the loss of a relationship and knew that in Zion I would find what I needed (many of us return to those special places that inspire and heal us). A friend dropped me off in the backcountry early one morning at a trailhead that would eventually lead back to Zion Canyon, 14 miles away.

While hiking I found myself revitalized and inspired. The scenery along the Lava Point Trail is spectacular, with almost a dozen canyons opening off the high, forested plateau along whose edge the trail traversed. An inspiration came to me that the place where I lived, near the desert resort of Palm Springs, California, would greatly benefit from a hiking club. The community needed an organized, safe entry into the desert, canyon, and mountain wilderness surrounding them.

Upon returning home, I placed a small ad in the paper and began drawing interested hikers into the makeshift beginnings of a reputable hiking club. Within three years we had over 1,000 members, and were conducting over 300 hikes per year for over 7,000 people. Much good has come from this endeavor, as way has led to way, both for me and for the club members. I attribute all these benefits to the inspirations offered me along the Lava Point Trail in Zion National Park.

I'm sure that readers have their own similar tales to tell. The point remains that going into nature is one way to uncover some of the meaning and purpose we all need to live fulfilling, stress-free lives.

RELEASE FROM EXCESSIVE DEMANDS
AND ATTACHMENT

Freedom is often a matter of what you can live without, not just what you can live with. Our society is devoted to the process of creating desire and perceived need, marketing the product, selling the customer. Consume rather than create. Many peoples' stress has come from having too many desires and not enough resources to obtain those desires. Instead of living in response to their own creative expressions and personal agenda, they have lived in reaction to what they believed they had to have, as created and articulated by society—have to get married, have to have this great job, have to have a house, this kind of car, so much money, etc.

Hiking takes us away from this onslaught of commercialism. On the trail, in the backcountry, we are keenly aware of the simplicity surrounding us, how we feel far less need for anything, as opposed to when we're in the city. Not having to think about whether to buy this or that, have this or that, not having to defend against any sales pressure, we feel less stress and are more relaxed. We are freed from having to make an endless chain of consumer decisions.

In nature, we see the simplicity of the world. Nature is just "there" to look at and enjoy—unconditionally. There is real peace in that. During a hike, we can assess some of the pressing issues in our lives and discover just how important they really are for us. We can more clearly evaluate what our needs are versus our wants, and what our best priorities are.

I've known people to decide to change careers after a hike, to get married (or to not get married), to choose to live somewhere else, or to give up a relationship that was unfulfilling. In nature it is easier to let go of what holds us back or what we've grown encumbered with. And with each release and detachment comes a lessening of our stress and a simplification of our lives. A journey through nature alerts us to how little it takes for us to enjoy ourselves and how much we fill up our lives with excess baggage.

RELEASE FROM RELATIONSHIP ISSUES

Many people discover that when they are away from someone they create stress with, the immediate absence of conflict encourages them to see the part they have played in creating the relationship stress. Away from their "person of issue," it is easier to understand the dynamics of their relationship, begin choosing new patterns of how to relate to the other person, and decide on how to communicate their new insights and action plans to this person.

Too many people never find the time out they need to resolve their relationship issues. They go from home to work and back home again, with entertainment distractions wedged in between. A hike into the backcountry offers a healing place to grow more aware of who we are in relationships. Nature is like a medieval church where one can claim sanctuary from the onslaughts of ones' oppressors, and hiking is what gets us through the door. It may be a work issue, a love issue, children, a significant other, but in nature we find the stillness we need to begin healing.

I am not offering specific solutions or options concerning relationship challenges. But I do offer a strong recommendation to take advantage of what hiking offers and use that "away" time, unhurried, revitalizing, and clarifying, to discover for ourselves what is going to make our relationships more fulfilling.

RELEASE FROM ABSENCE OF LOVE

Of the many sources of personal stress, the absence of love in our lives is a cause often overlooked. The natural retreat that a hike gives us is a good opportunity to look at the ways in which love enters our lives.

We interact with love in three ways. We accept love and support from others; we give love, comfort, and support to ourselves in the form of self-love; and we offer love and support to other people. A hike offers us a good time to evaluate how we are dealing with these three aspects of love. Our minds are clearer when we are out in nature, and the very act of taking ourselves on a hike draws our attention to how we are treating ourselves.

In the first aspect of love, we need to assess if we are open to receiving love and support from others. Do we acknowledge our need to be loved? What do we do when love is offered? For thirteen years I worked with teenage alcoholics and addicts, and discovered that many people were attempting to love them and support their efforts at recovery, but it was they who often shut the door and did not trust love when it was given. People begin growing only when they are open to the love offered them.

The next challenge is to see if we are loving ourselves, being our own best friend. Are we taking care of our needs, tending to our lives, setting acceptable limits on the claims others make on us? By not judging, condemning, attacking, or belittling ourselves, we are practicing self-love. More importantly, by fulfilling our own needs, giving ourselves needed rest, recreation, and the love of friends when we need it, growing in physical, mental, emotional, and spiritual well-being, we assure that love is satisfactorily flowing in our lives.

Finally, are we loving others, freely, in ways that assure their highest good, in ways that are not controlling, conditional, and judgmental? Do we freely give attention and respect other people's rights? Do we offer some form of service to the community, our neighbors, relatives, friends?

Within this whole system of love, if we are accepting love from others, loving ourselves, and offering love to others, our stress levels will dramatically lessen.

PERSONALITY TYPES AND STRESS MANAGEMENT

Psychologists often use a personality assessment tool known as the Myers-Briggs Type Indicator. Using this assessment, most people are categorized as one of four personality types that indicates how they create, react to, and solve their stress problems. The four types successfully deal with stress in ways that hiking directly relates to.

Intuitive-Thinking

One personality type manages stress by becoming more competent and starting a new project. For these people, the skills gained by hiking—being in the backcountry alone, solving whatever challenges arise, learning to be confident in nature and the wilderness, discovering, often for the first time, the wonders of the great outdoors—all support their successful dealing with stress.

Intuitive-Feeling
Another personality type needs nurturing and a new quest. Hiking offers them the peace of the outdoors, the quiet beauty, the quest for the deeper discovery of self often found in nature. By hiking, they fulfill a multitude of needs by nurturing themselves. They treat themselves to an outing into nature and the benefits of hiking, they test new skills, and they discover, like explorers of old, the great canyon country of Utah, or the mountain expanses of the Rockies, and a host of other natural wonders found only by hiking into the heart of these spectacular places. Hiking with friends provides a needed support network on the trail. People will often feel safe sharing intimacies and secrets with a stranger during a casual encounter. Perhaps a train ride or during a long airport delay. Repeated hiking with buddies met on the trail by being part of the same hiking club or group encourages this type of bonding. Once your stories have been shared, the bond deepens by continually hiking together, and people soon loosen up and discover that they have made potentially life long friends with folks they otherwise would not have known or considered.

People from diverse cultural and economic backgrounds meet on the trail and discover a commonality of values and personality that excites them as they become fast friends. These new friendships carry over into other activities and areas in their lives.

Sensor-Judger

Another personality type finds stress relief by being appreciated and being included in a project. Hiking fulfills their needs when they ask others to share with them the goodness of the land, the benefits of hiking, perhaps by asking others to accompany them out into nature, introducing them to what hiking has to offer, through scouting, joining a hiking club, or becoming a hike leader, etc.

Sensor-Perceiver

The fourth personality type needs shared experiences, change, and novelty to reduce their stress levels. Hiking in a group, with a club, with friends, or with a favorite companion provides the shared experience they need. Just discovering a new trail every week satisfies the need for change and novelty. They soon find that nature offers incredible diversity, each trail being a whole new world awaiting discovery.

MANAGING STRESS BY HIKING

Hundreds of people have shared with me how hiking has helped them overcome their stress. Be it surviving the death of a loved one, struggling with marital and other relationship problems, making a job/career change, life change, or place of living change, dealing with one's unmet needs, or introducing a badly needed exercise regimen into a person's lifestyle, hiking offers very real, consistent, and timely solutions.

Hiking provides both the setting and often the means for people to formulate stress management techniques that work. For many sedentary Americans, estimated to number over 50 million, hiking is not the hour-of-duty in the gym. It's fun. It takes place in the stimulating, ever-changing, and scenic outdoors. It enables its practitioner to burn more than the minimum number of calories, it keeps one's interest, and it definitely isn't boring. Lessons in geology, botany, geography and a host of other sciences are often available to hikers on every journey. Nature itself is the classroom.

Successful stress management is a natural consequence of hiking, at a minimum, two to three times a month. Take to the trail—and discover this often overlooked benefit that comes from hiking.

THE PHYSICAL BENEFITS OF HIKING

Conditioning and Maintaining
a Healthy Body

"From a medical standpoint hiking has it all: great exercise,
spiritual highs, and a feeling of accomplishment.

To achieve cardiopulmonary exercise in such a pleasurable
way as hiking is unique. Whether enjoying the solitude of
nature or sharing the trail with friends, the relaxation and
enjoyment are both rewarding and therapeutic.

To reach a goal, enjoy exercise, find an emotional escape,
or just have fun, hiking encompasses them all."

—R. William Hilty, M.D.

HIKING IS A NATURAL FORM OF EXERCISE

During the fitness boom in the '70s when gym memberships soared, experts suggested at least twenty minutes of aerobic exercise three times a week. A workout on alternate days was ideal, providing more cardiovascular activity and toning of muscles. Almost overnight, we had fat-free chocolate chip cookies, low-calorie candy bars, and semi-healthy potato chips. We ate, not really enjoying the taste, but knowing we were doing something good for our bodies. But the food became bland, the workouts at the gym for many were boring, and the exercise equipment that once held a place of honor in our homes was banished to the garage.

Many people lack motivation or determination to get into shape. New Year's resolutions are busted before the end of January and most Americans sulk around, feeling sorry for themselves for accepting a sedentary life on the couch munching potato chips. Everyone agrees that exercise and watching what you eat are the best ways to maintain a healthy weight and boost energy. The problem is sticking with it.

Hikers say they have no problem sticking with it. Every hike is different. Hiking brings variety. That same old trail takes on a different look and feel depending on what time of the year it is, who your hiking partners are, and what type of mood you're in. Moods and attitudes change, too. Be a kid again. Climb over rocks, leap over streams, laugh, and play. Don't be shy. Isn't everyone young at heart? The greatest reward is that every hike, regardless how many times you took that same trail, is different. Flowers bloom where only green stems sprouted from the soil before. Branches fall, making way for new tree growth. Barrel cactus or ocotillo, once dry and brittle in the summer, beam with bright purple and orange buds in the spring. Every step taken allows the hiker to experience a different type of workout.

Life gets a little better sitting at the top of a mountain peak, savoring the magnificent view of the valley several thousand feet below. Or maybe it's overlooking a forest of dense evergreen trees. Perhaps the landscape is tinted with pink and lavender hues of a setting sun across a barren desert floor. Whatever the view is—life is good.

Problems that once seemed heavy on the mind vanish. Stress that once caused headaches and a painful back and shoulders is gone. When hiking is incorporated into a regular exercise regime, extra pounds also seem to melt away. That's what hiking does for the mind and body.

No matter how often you hike, look for exhilarating challenges. Try hiking 8 miles through sand, and feel the gentle pull of calf and thigh muscles as they are toning themselves. Sometimes using your arms and upper body is necessary to hoist yourself over boulders or scramble up and over a small rock formation. All movement gives muscles a chance to exercise and strengthen.

Regardless how much a person works out, any level of hiking or walking benefits the body. Whether it be a ten-minute brisk walk around the block or an all-day trek up a steep trail, hiking conditions the body by burning calories and toning all leg and thigh muscles. Swing your arms and you'll really get your heart pumping and blood circulating.

HIKING IS A CARDIOVASCULAR WORKOUT

Hikers enjoy a good cardiovascular or heart-pumping workout, especially on longer, more strenuous hikes. Hiking is an aerobic exercise, a slow buildup of raising the heart rate for a minimum of twenty to thirty minutes. Aerobic exercise burns fat, circulates blood, pumps the heart, heats up muscles, and stretches the lungs. When the heart rate increases, it slightly increases the rate at which it's pumping blood throughout the muscles. It also raises the metabolic rate so foods are digested quickly and used for energy.

Hiking, similar to climbing stairs, tones leg muscles. But unlike being stuck on a stair-climber machine in a gym, hiking is a form of exercise done in a pristine outdoor setting. So many hikers say they don't feel like they are working out because they are having fun, enjoying the view, and breathing fresh air. Nature is the greatest distraction from even thinking about exercise!

Developing a passion to hike virtually assures fitness for life and a healthy weight maintenance program. More importantly, hikers shed unwanted calories and toxins and give the mind a mental workout. Sweating on a tough hike during a warm day also releases toxins and opens pores.

Hikers who want a greater workout can climb a steeper trail, increase their pace, or lengthen their stride.

HIKING BURNS CALORIES AND HELPS YOU LOSE WEIGHT

Fitness and health experts suggest aerobics to maintain weight and burn unwanted pounds. More than 400 calories per hour can be burned in a six-hour moderate hike, according to fitness experts—that's almost 2,500 calories used during an enjoyable outing in nature. The amount of calories burned varies depending on what shape you are in, how fast or slow your hiking pace is, and whether you are hiking uphill or down. The following is a breakdown of calories burned on an average hike:

	Elevation Gain (ft)	Miles	Calories burned per hour
Easy	0-500	4-7	350-400
Moderate	500-1,800	6-10	400-450
Strenuous	1,800-5,000	8-15	450-500

Hiking also raises a person's metabolic rate for twenty-four to thirty-six hours after hiking. This elevated rate increases the fat-burning function of the body, ensuring even more calories are used. If a person were to just take a short hike of several hours some other time during that same week and eat moderate meals with no additional above-normal intake of calories, that individual could lose one pound per week!

I know many people who took up hiking for, among other reasons, the support it gives toward successful weight loss. Many people who are hiking for this purpose begin doing moderate to strenuous hikes several times a week, or 20 to 25 miles per week. They experience weight loss of from two to three pounds per week, until they reach certain lower levels of weight that their body finds comfortable . . . the so-called "set point." Then hiking becomes more of a weight maintenance program. Regular hikers are fit.

A hiker in the club I belong to began to hike weekly in April. By July he had lost six inches around his middle, shed thirty pounds, and looked years younger with a beaming, joyful, and energized face. From his perspective he had also lost "years" from the aging process, feeling and looking ten years younger!

Another hiker I know spent a summer in Boulder, Colorado. In his words, "I was at my highest weight ever, even though it was only twenty pounds over my weight when I was in high school. But I felt weighed down, uncomfortable, and uneasy about myself. So I began eating less fat and more fruit, vegetables, and pastas, and I began hiking three times a week. In a month I had gone from 150 to 137 pounds, but still couldn't break through that "set point" weight of 137. A little more hiking and I finally broke through, down to 132 pounds. What a difference! The moment I went under 135, I felt a surge of energy well up in me and infuse even my mental state with the feelings I had at twenty years old. I had shed enough pounds so that energy I once used for carrying excess weight now went into my feeling better and even more creative. Since then, by enjoying several regular hikes per week, I've kept my weight at 132 pounds and I still feel highly energized. Hiking proved so much fun that I never dreaded or felt unmotivated about sticking to my weekly hikes. In fact, I think there is a 'feeling good' cycle that regular hiking creates. After each hike I reflect on how good, energized, and light I feel, and how uplifting my experiences on the trail were. The more I feel this way, the more committed I am to constantly feeling this good. The alternative just isn't a viable option."

The combination of increased exercise, reduced stress levels, being out in fresh air, and being rewarded with countless beautiful scenes acts to calm people in such a way that the individual feels less urgency to eat or to eat the larger quantities once thought necessary for feeling good. The greatly

increased calorie/fat burn, stress reduction, enhanced tranquillity, and exercise all prove a powerful regimen for excellent
weight loss and body firming and toning. The longer the
hike, the more calories are burned.

Cold Weather Burns More Calories
The body also burns calories at a much faster rate (perhaps
40 percent faster) in weather that approaches 32 degrees
Fahrenheit. So even if you are living in a climate not usually
associated with winter hiking, you can still hike trails free
from snow or with levels of less than six inches, or you can
snowshoe; the body will not only burn up those calories, but
do so much more quickly. The colder temperature forces the
body to maintain itself at a core temperature of 98.6 degrees
Fahrenheit, so it is forced to heat up the body against the
cold by employing a faster metabolic rate.

The city of Boulder, Colorado, has dozens of miles of hiking trails in the mountains west of the city known as the
Boulder Mountain Parks. Rangers tell me that during a
normal winter, the hiking trails in the park are used
throughout the winter. Snow levels just don't get that deep.
So remember that there are possibilities for hiking winter
trails after all, even in the ski state of Colorado!

Hot Weather Burns More Calories Too
The counterpart to calories burning faster at colder temperatures is that the heat of desert hiking forces the body
to also increase calorie burn rates, because the cooling
mechanism of the body must work overtime.

A trail in the Palm Springs, California, area known for its
steep ascent is the Skyline Trail, also known as the Cactus-to-Clouds Trail, in the San Jacinto Mountains. San

Jacinto is the steepest peak in North America, rising 10,000 feet in less than 7 miles. No other peak rises so high so fast. The trail begins at about 500 feet and zigzags its way up a steep mountain through thick brush, then climbs higher up over yet another mountain ridge. In all, it's 11 miles long, and with elevation gains of 10,500 feet, it's one of the most demanding hikes in America.

I have scaled the Skyline Trail twice. The first time I made it to the top in under nine hours. I shaved another two hours hiking the trail the second time around. But after each experience, I felt fantastic and energized when I reached the end of the trail. On top of the feeling of euphoria, I had worked my calf and thigh muscles with every lunge up the mountain. My legs stretched as I carried myself up the sometimes very steep terrain. The backpack filled with water and food added more weight to the hike, increasing my heart rate.

Carrying Weight Also Burns More Calories
Most hikers strap a pack to their backs, or some prefer the around-the-waist version. Depending on how much food, drink, and equipment is taken, daypacks can be a hiker's free weights on the trail, for both toning and strengthening muscles. Another benefit of carrying some sort of pack is that it helps in burning the fat. However, most dayhikers do not require heavy equipment. But no matter how much food, water, or other items you bring along, it all helps you achieve a more effective workout. Some hikers choose to supplement a hiking regimen with some upper-body and back-firming exercises to strengthen the shoulders and back, which could make carrying a backpack more comfortable.

A very experienced desert hiker I know, who has trekked thousands of miles during his life, always carried a fifteen- to twenty-pound pack. Inside, he stored climbing rope, gallons of water, a first aid kit, a snake bite kit, a pocket knife, a folder filled with maps and hiking books, plus other items hidden deep in the crevices of his pack. At the beginning of each hike, he'd hoist the heavy burlap pack over his shoulders onto his back and strap it tightly around his muscle-toned abdomen.

HIKING HELPS REDUCE CHOLESTEROL

Experts have long known that people with high blood pressure risk getting atherosclerosis, a cholesterol-clogging of blood vessels commonly called hardening of the arteries. A hiker I know has lowered her cholesterol levels from over 300 to under 170, and she attributes this to her combination of weekly hiking coupled with a change in diet. It seems that many hikers, because they are changing their lifestyle and exercise habits by hiking, feel less of an urge to eat fatty foods and to overeat. On the trail, you can't afford to stuff in a lot of junk food, because the body then takes needed blood for leg muscles during the hike and redistributes it to the digestive tract for digestion. The feeling hikers get is uncomfortable enough that most opt to eat lightly or moderately during a hike. Hiking has its own built-in mechanism for helping hikers kick the high-fat foods craze.

CONDITION YOURSELF FOR HIKING

To get in shape could mean taking aerobic classes, bicycling, or jogging. Leg strength can be enhanced by various exercises, either at home or at a gym, but just by walking longer distances and by actually hiking, your total physical conditioning will greatly improve.

Conditioning yourself for hiking is as important to the success of a hike as wearing the appropriate shoes. Never venture out on a hike without knowing how many miles you want to travel, how much elevation gain there is, if any, and what type of terrain you will be hiking through. Of course, always be prepared for the unexpected. But more importantly, know how far your body can go.

Conditioning means preparing your heart, lungs, and legs on smaller hikes before attempting a longer or more strenuous hike you would like to do in the future. Even the most skilled hikers, before attempting to do a much larger climb or hike, train by duplicating the conditions of the proposed hike.

Try to train in climates to which your body and mind are accustomed. But be prepared to change your training routine if, for example, you're used to hiking in the desert and suddenly have an urge to hike 14,495-foot Mount Whitney, located in the Sierras of Northern California, with colder temperatures. Train wisely.

Be prepared to use all your body strength during any hike, to hop over boulders, climb under or over fallen trees, or cross streams or creeks, if necessary. The body should be in shape to handle any situation you may encounter on the trail.

I remember a new hiker who was in her fifties, starting out on 4- to 5-mile hikes. Within less than a year, just by hiking at least once a week, she had graduated into doing 8,000-foot-elevation-gain hikes, with distances of up to 15 miles. Hiking produces better conditioning for hiking.

CHALLENGE YOUR PHYSICAL LIMITS BY HIKING

"The element of risk keeps us sharp. If we take the risk, we can keep ourselves young," stated an article in *Shape* magazine. Those dedicated to hiking push themselves to more challenging hikes.

Roger and Maria Keezer, both in their sixties, go out at least twice a week plus every weekend. An added kicker: these two only do hikes of 10 miles or more. "It's great exercise. In the beginning I couldn't go 5 miles without huffing and puffing. Now, we are in very good shape. We like to go out there and do really strenuous hikes. We'll never stop," Maria said. Hiking is almost like a "good addiction," the Keezers said. Something about inhaling fresh air, walking to unspoiled areas, or just being alone with nature pushes the Keezers to hike more and more.

Or could it be they have lost weight and say they have more energy today than they ever did before they started hiking three years ago? Maria has lost twenty pounds since hiking, dropping from a size twelve to a fit size six.

"I only wish everyone would give it a try. I didn't think we would get so serious about it. It's a very important part of our life," she said. The incredible drop in body fat and inches is just one of the many reasons the Keezers love to hike.

Simply put, hikers choose to hike as a form of exercise. Time on a mountain is time well spent. Wanda Neste, owner of Gold's Gym in Palm Springs, California, began hiking after she had a bad day at the office. Today, she has graduated from dayhikes to overnight alpine mountaineering. She has climbed Tanzania's 19,340-foot Kilimanjaro in Africa and a host of other demanding peaks.

Carl Garczynski has climbed Mount Rainier in Washington—14,410 feet—twenty-three times and Mount Jefferson in Oregon—10,497 feet—thirteen times. Last year, in his mid-fifties, he set out to climb Mount Kilimanjaro in Africa. Three years ago, he reached the 26,000-foot level of 29,028-foot Mount Everest and would have been the oldest person to climb the summit at the time of his ascent. He has encouraged an entire generation to get physical. He regularly speaks to senior citizen and hiking groups about his hiking and mountaineering feats. "Hiking has a mind-body coordination," he said. "You really disassociate yourself from other things and are forced to concentrate on what you are doing. It's more inward-thinking rather that outward. On a hike you choose to be there."

Garczynski hikes to stay in shape. During an average of thirty minutes in the weight room plus forty-five minutes on a stationary bike or stair-climber, he said he burns between 600 to 700 calories. In comparison, several hours of hiking melts up to 1,000 calories. Garczynski, for many years a weather forecaster for the National Weather Service near Palm Springs, California, has made a lifetime commitment to outdoor recreation, hiking, and running.

EXERCISE SAFELY BY HIKING

Hikes are a form of exercise; they require us to use different muscles for going uphill and down. Some people are in such good shape that they think nothing of doing strenuous hikes for three days in a row. But most people would do well to take a day of rest in between hikes, or follow a strenuous hike with a moderate or easy one. Hiking is not a contest to see how many miles we can log or how far we can go. Hiking, instead, is an exercise tool we can use to balance our lives, enjoying this outdoor pursuit rather than merely enduring it.

Some hikers complain of knee problems when going long distances downhill. Such people should consult an exercise or physical therapist. I have found that when certain tendons and muscles around the knee are weak, they more easily give out when coming downhill. Some people can remedy this condition by regular workouts with exercise machines designed to strengthen the knee, thigh and calf areas. What these machines really do is build up those muscles that work the knee, allowing the hiker to take downhill slopes more easily.

Other physical conditions resulting from hiking might occur. Sometimes a good podiatrist can help remedy foot-related conditions. Physical therapists and chiropractors are also excellent resources for maintaining health and fitness when it is related to muscle and bone stresses.

I've known a number of hikers with hip or knee replacements who experienced little or no difficulty returning to hiking on a regular basis. In fact, the exercise of hiking is a strong conditioning regimen for the body at any age. There are stories of people in their eighties who still hike in relative comfort while enjoying all the benefits that hiking offers.

All forms of hikes require some movement and energy. The body, constantly in motion, always alert, is always challenging itself on a hike. It's also enjoyable, safe and beneficial. Dayhiking is, in many ways, one of the safest of all athletic exercise pursuits.

I know few dayhikers who have ever injured themselves on the trail, and those who do often are not experienced hikers, but go without having the proper equipment for the trail they attempt doing. I participate in a hiking club in which just two sprained ankles resulted after 7,000 people hiked a total of more than 70,000 miles. And one of these accidents came as a result of someone wearing improper footwear. Dayhiking is just the normal human experience of walking through nature. Simple, uncomplicated—natural.

Enjoy Exercise by Hiking

If you've never hiked before, give it a try. You *will* like it. By pushing yourself out of your comfort zone, you'll get a tremendous rush of energy and it will build an enormous amount of self-esteem. If you are a hiker, keep it up and aim for new challenges to improve your skills.

Regardless of your hiking ability, remember that you are doing good things for your body. Through walks, the body tones itself, the heart pumps stronger, and energy is replenished. Hiking is the best form of exercise I know. As a member of a gym for several years, I know it's tough to keep motivated to exercise sometimes. But I always think of the wonderful places I've visited on foot. I remember how good my body and soul felt as I breathed in the fresh air and saw incredible sights. Hiking is freedom.

THE HIKING COMMUNITY

Getting to Know Your Fellow Travelers

"Anything that creates emotional ties between human beings . . . Everything that leads to important shared action creating such common feelings . . . On them the structure of human society in good measure rests."

—*Sigmund Freud to Albert Einstein*

BUILDING COMMUNITY

America is a nation on the go. Nearly one in four of us moves each year to a different living situation. Economic upheavals, personal changes in marital status, the quest for new opportunities, and the job search all contribute to this migration pattern Americans sum up in one word: mobility.

But mobility has its price. Mother Teresa, during one of her journeys through the United States, was asked about her impressions. She surprised her questioner by observing what a lonely place America was. Billy Graham has reiterated her claim with one of his own, that loneliness is *the* pressing, unspoken issue for Americans. Ironically, with our vast capacity and capability for communication, both mass and individual, we are perhaps better talking *at* or *about* each other than *with* each other.

An entire generation grew up as victims of the "latchkey phenomenon"—with absentee parents, or parents too busy making a living or watching television, who don't share and interact with their children. We are a nation high on mistrust and low on tolerance, acceptance, and real community participation. Sigmund Freud once stated that real community built around strong emotional bonds is created through shared experience. Sharing a common task sets the stage for sharing common feelings.

Several years ago, I participated in starting and developing a hiking club in the Palm Springs, California, area. In a few short years more than 1,200 people had joined. But it was not the numbers that gave me real satisfaction; rather, it was the creation of a "hiking community" that was most uplifting.

From the very start, volunteers participated in the building and running of the organization. Brochures were designed and distributed, hike leaders trained, schedules published, hikes taken—from fifty the first year to three hundred by the end of the third. Still, it was the community aspect that was central to both the club's success and the fulfillment of the members.

People discovered each other, kindred spirits who loved nature, loved to hike, explore, and even grow together into other outdoor sport enthusiasts—mountain climbing, camping, river rafting, backpacking, and rock climbing. Shared challenges, scenic settings absent of the hurried, cluttered artifacts of civilization, and the common experience of hiking through the wilderness all helped create a "hiking community," people bonded in their common love of nature, open to anyone who shared that same love.

As a result of hiking with the club, people experienced numerous benefits beyond the physical aspects of exercise and improved health. New friends were made—people who could be invited on a hike any day of the week. In this way, smaller social circles of friends evolved for the purpose of both hiking and sharing other common interests. For people new to the desert area, these benefits were quite valuable. The easy pace and open spaces found along the trail encouraged hikers to share life stories, concerns, feelings, and personal issues. People from different walks of life, greatly unrelated when seen in the context of the workplace, made friends with one another, while learning the unique perspective offered by each other's different backgrounds. The building of community gave support to members and a feeling of "home" in the sometimes hostile natural environment of the desert.

THE EXTENDED HIKING COMMUNITY

Conservation groups like the Sierra Club offer an impressive array of outdoor trips. These include backpacking, base camp, lodge, family, and service trips, both in and outside the United States. By meeting other hiking enthusiasts, not only on club or organization outings but on any guided trip vacation, you "run the risk" of making lifelong hiking friends with whom you can plan other trips.

The American Volkssport Association is a dynamic organization of over 550 clubs nationwide that "promotes physical fitness and good health by providing fun-filled, safe exercise in a stress-free environment. . . . Walking (hiking) is the most popular of all the volkssporting (German for "the sport of the people") activities, but there are also biking, swimming, cross-country skiing, snowshoeing, and more. All events are noncompetitive with you, the volkssporter, choosing the sport, the distance, and the pace. Events take place throughout the year, all around the country. Historic and scenic sites are selected for your enjoyment. Walking (hiking) events provide a special opportunity for family members to interact without the interruption of the phone, television, and doorbell. Children enjoy the trails as much as their parents and grandparents do. Students, scouts, and community organizations often participate as groups.

Some college extensions offer seminars or classes in outdoor recreation, hiking, and backpacking. Recreational Equipment Inc. (REI), an outdoor gear cooperative, conducts outdoor classes. You'll be surprised how many places are connected in some way to outdoor recreation. The payoff, however, is in actually enjoying the outdoors. Seeing all those scenic and wild places in documentaries or in books in no way matches the pleasure of actually hiking.

Throughout the United States there are hundreds of hiking clubs that exist to bring together people who enjoy not only hiking, but almost any outdoor activity. Like the network of trails that interconnect across America, hiking clubs offer their members the opportunity to get into the wilderness, from the Atlantic to the Pacific, from Canada to Mexico, in perhaps every national, state, and local park, national forest, and wilderness area. These guided hikes are safe, done in small, friendly groups, and usually require just the interest of the participant and proper equipment.

If a person is traveling to Tucson for a winter vacation, they will find the very active Southern Arizona Hiking Club, with a membership of over 2,000 and offering at least sixty hikes a month. A trip to the Eastern seaboard connects them with the Appalachian Trail Conference or the Appalachian Mountain Club, groups that hike the more than 1,000 miles of the famed Appalachian Trail. In other parts of America, hikers find such clubs as the Kansas and Iowa Trails Council, the Pacific Crest Trail Conference, the San Francisco-based Bay Area Ridge Trail Council, and many others.

The hiking and outdoor community is growing fast. Demographics indicate that people moving into what was once known as "middle age," the fifties-plus surge from the baby boomers' generation, are turning to hiking and the outdoors for their exercise and re-creation needs. Hiking clubs offer a friendly and very social way to connect with one's fellow travelers.

A hiking friend of mine offers this testimony of her experience in the hiking club she joined. "I am a married, fifty-five-year-old grandmother of five. Why would I join a hiking club at my age, become a hike leader for the club, and want to recruit others to do the same?

"For me, I have come full circle with the happy memories and love for the outdoors I experienced in childhood. My family fished, camped, and hiked during my growing-up years, spending family vacations in Yellowstone, the Grand Tetons, and other somewhat untouched wilderness areas. Mammoth Lakes in California was familiar territory for long weekend outings.

"But my parents divorced when I was in my late teens, my mother died when I was nineteen, and I married my high school sweetheart when I was twenty. My husband had never spent time in the outdoors; for him, roughing it was a motel room without room service! It seemed that my youthful enjoyment of the beauty of nature was to remain in my childhood.

"We raised two children, grown and married now. Over the years my husband and I were just too busy with our family and his business; I returned to college in my forties. We eventually moved to the desert around Palm Springs, California, for our semi-retirement. Just six weeks after moving, I responded to a notice for an orientation meeting of the Coachella Valley Hiking Club. Because I used to hike as a kid, I decided to go.

"A wonderful presentation was given about the club, along with a slide show of some of the beautiful seventy-five-plus trails that the club hiked in the desert and surrounding mountains. Slides were also shown of the club's yearly trip to Zion National Park in Utah. Equipment was discussed, along with safety and desert hiking conditions.

"I was hooked. I joined the club, bought some sturdy boots, called to get on a hike, and hit the trail. Now I lead hikes for the club, help in administrative work, enjoy a trail or two weekly, and tell everyone I meet about the wonderful advantages of hiking and the club I belong to. I've been to Zion twice, and recently participated in a club hiking and camping trip down the Havasupai Trail into the Grand Canyon. And wonder of wonders—my husband bought a pair of hiking boots and together we enjoyed hiking many trails through Switzerland.

"I have come full circle with my love for hiking and being in the outdoors. I have come full circle with my past, enjoyed meeting and hiking with terrific people, reaped the benefits of traveling the outdoors, fulfilled my passion for hiking, and relived memories of my long-ago childhood."

If there is anything about hiking that is less than very upbeat, it is the momentary frustration felt by people who discover the joys of hiking later in life. They wished that they had hit the trails beginning in their teens and twenties rather than waiting until their retirement. Had they done so, perhaps joining in various volunteer projects along the way, they would have enjoyed a lifetime of hiking with friends who shared their interest and enthusiasm. But no matter; once they do discover hiking, they involve themselves quickly with great energy to enjoy all the many hikes that are still theirs to discover.

WHAT HIKING CLUBS ARE ALL ABOUT

Hiking clubs offer their members diverse outdoor experiences centered around hiking. Hiking clubs sponsor both local and out-of-area trips. The larger clubs travel to Europe, South America, and many parts of North America in their quest for adventure. These trips are cost effective, with only a small service fee and each member paying for their own food and lodging.

Outdoor Activities
In addition to its hiking trips, The Mountaineers (located in Seattle, Washington, with 15,000 members) offers backpacking trips, car camping, naturalist hikes, photography outings, family outings, folk dancing, singles' programs, foreign trips, bicycling, skiing, climbing, alpine scrambling, sea kayaking, and sailing.

The Colorado Mountain Club (with almost 10,000 members organized in chapters throughout the state, including Aspen, Boulder, Denver, Pikes Peak, and the San Juans) offers over 2,500 activities annually. Each chapter sponsors its own activities, but hiking is at the top of the list, along with climbing Colorado's famous "fourteeners" (peaks over 14,000 feet high), skiing, rock climbing, snowshoeing, and bicycling.

The Coachella Valley Hiking Club (in Southern California, with over 1,000 members), the hiking club I'm a member of, offers trips to Zion National Park, Utah; Mammoth Lakes, Kings Canyon National Park, and Mount Whitney, California; Colorado; and the Grand Canyon, Arizona.

Volunteer Activities

Clubs also offer members the opportunity to do trail and environment cleanups, trail building and maintenance, perhaps docent work at local outdoor centers, and outreach education. For instance, activities of The Colorado Mountain Club include campground hosting, research and field work, trail construction and landscaping, interpretive tour guides, and botany and forest work.

The American Hiking Society, though not a hiking club, staffs the National Hiking Information Center and its online counterpart that provides resources covering advocacy, planning, and funding for trail proponents and destination information for hikers. The AHS also sponsors Volunteer Vacations, a program where teams of ten to twelve volunteers are equipped and sent into "some of America's most remote backcountry for one- and two-week vacations to renovate and clear existing trails, and build new ones. The program offers an inexpensive way to visit a new part of the country, work with your hands, and feel good about giving something back."

Many hiking clubs participate in the activities of the National Trails Day. This is held usually during the first week of June, and gives any outdoor club or organization the chance to work on a trail or environmental project in their own back yard. The American Hiking Society, for example, sponsors activities for National Trails Day, "America's largest celebration of the outdoors," each June with hikes, trail repair and cleanups, equipment demonstrations, and even outdoor cooking classes.

The American Hiking Society also publishes *Helping Out in the Outdoors*, a directory of internships and volunteer positions on America's public lands, including national parks and forests, nature preserves, state parks and forests, and environmental education centers. In all, more than 2,000 volunteer opportunities are listed, including campground hosts, backcountry trail patrols, archaeological assistants, wildlife assistants, tree planters, interpretive naturalists, fire lookouts, tour guides, visitor center receptionists, and photographers.

Hiking clubs often coordinate with governmental agencies in trail maintenance and related projects. The U.S. Forest Service and the Bureau of Land Management are two agencies that clubs primarily deal with in their efforts to build or maintain new or existing trails. Colorado's premier outdoor service organization, Volunteers for Outdoor Colorado, includes such activities as campground hosting, research and field work, trail work, construction and landscaping, interpretive tour guides, botany and forest work, and outdoor recreation.

Government agencies also offer volunteer opportunities to the general public. The Forest Service sponsors individuals as trail, camp, and wilderness hosts. The Forest Service pays a small stipend and offers some housing and uniforms to people who, most often during the busy summer, travel the wilderness trails helping hikers, giving trail information, and the like. People I know who have done this kind of "work" love the opportunity to be outdoors for most of the summer, meeting a variety of people from all over the country as they walk the backcountry trails while staying fit and trim from all that hiking!

Member Services
You can find out where the nearest hiking club is by contacting the American Hiking Society (see appendix A, Hiking Clubs) and asking for information about hiking clubs affiliated with them. While not a hiking club in the traditional sense, the American Hiking Society has a wealth of information about trails, hiking, and hiking organizations. The organization publishes the *American Hiker* magazine and the *National Directory of Trail Organizations.*

Several years ago, I wrote an article for a national hiking magazine about starting your own hiking club. In the several months after the story appeared, I received between fifty and seventy inquiries from people who wanted to do just that. I shared with them the steps I took to start a hiking club in my area and hoped that they would follow suit. Readers of this book can do the same if no hiking club or group is nearby where you live.

Even if the clubs listed in your area are not conveniently located near you, they will be able to direct you to one that is. Once you've found a hiking club you're interested in, ask for their club brochure and membership information. Like many hiking clubs, The Mountaineers offers prospective members an information meeting showing slides of various club activities. Many clubs allow prospective members to take a few hikes with them before deciding whether to join.

Once you join, you receive an activities program (The Mountaineers' July '96 edition was 48 pages long!) highlighting what outdoor activities the club offers. As a member you can expect some sort of orientation meeting where the organization, activities, and other club functions are discussed. For example, The Mountaineers' hiking outings are graded as easy, moderate, or strenuous, with ten to thirty hikes planned for each weekend; many midweek hikes are also scheduled.

Training Courses
Members do not have to be fully experienced to join a hiking club. The Colorado Mountain Club, for example, specializes in alpine mountaineering, and conducts outdoor schools in hiking, wilderness trekking, backpacking, rock climbing, cross-country skiing, wilderness survival, mountaineering, ice climbing, leadership, and winter camping. The Mountaineers conducts courses in alpine scrambling, backcountry skiing, backpacking, canoeing, first aid, snowshoeing, environmental issues, and whitewater kayaking. Hiking clubs offer people the chance to enjoy the outdoors in a safe and social way, learning new skills to build on what they already know. Members in turn can give back through becoming trip leaders and event sponsors, sharing with their community the joys of the great outdoors.

The new hiker should be especially aware of attempting hikes that match their conditioning level. If a person has never hiked or hikes only infrequently, he or she should try a beginning or easy hike of 3 to 5 miles, with elevation gains of under 800 feet. If the person finds such a hike too easy, a moderate hike of 6 to 9 miles, with elevation gains of under 1,800 feet, can next be attempted. What is important is that the hiker is comfortable with the length and kind of hike they go on.

In time the average hiker graduates into being able to do strenuous hikes of 9 to 14 miles, with 3,000-plus feet in elevation gain. However, for comfort and because of their own time constraints, physical considerations, etc., many hikers sometimes choose to stay at a moderate hike level. If the hiking club offers other outdoor activities, hikers often expand their interests to perhaps include rock climbing, backpacking, camping, skiing, mountaineering, etc. It's a lot of fun moving into other outdoor experiences with hiking buddies from the hiking club you're in—almost like going through school together.

Hiking clubs offer a diversity of activities at various times of the week, day, and year. You might choose from an offering of sunrise hikes, full-moon rambles, geology, botany, or photography hikes, midafternoon into evening hikes, weekend trips or longer club trips to adventurous, scenic destinations like Yosemite, Zion, Glacier, or Yellowstone National Parks.

What is so rewarding about all these experiences are the great people you can share your love of nature with and the rewarding natural beauty found with any hike. Most of the people who have accompanied me on our hiking club's five-day hike through Zion National Park remark that it was one of the most enjoyable trips they have ever taken.

HIKING WITH GROUPS OF FRIENDS

It is safer to hike with someone else than alone. Many people would hike more often if they knew others they could share the trail with. This is a good reason for joining a hiking club, or going on hikes with organizations like the Sierra Club, YMCA/YWCA, or your local parks and recreation department. Some outdoor shops also sponsor hikes. You might also place a notice in hiking shops to discover potential hiking partners, or encourage the local sporting goods store to begin sponsoring weekly hiking outings. Experience has shown me that by building up this network of fellow hikers, one can more easily create a hiking lifestyle than by hiking solo. By hiking with others, you will eventually meet enough people who match up with your time schedule to be able to arrange to hike in small groups together.

What is important is that people who want to start hiking, people who have not hiked for years but want to begin again, or people who now rarely hike begin discovering the wonderful joys and benefits of traveling through nature while hiking. *Are We Having Fun Yet?* by Brian Baird (The Mountaineers, 1995) gives advice on enjoying the outdoors with partners, families, and groups, so that, rather than letting the challenges of the wilderness create relationship problems, we can build relationships outdoors.

HIKING ALONE

Hiking is one of the few sports that a single person can really enjoy doing alone. There are times when one should hike with other people, when hiking with others is more enjoyable than when hiking alone. But there are also times when hiking alone offers a special setting in which a person might find their needs fulfilled. All the benefits of hiking apply whether one hikes in a group or solo. For people in professions and job settings that demand a great deal of people interaction and/or service, being able to be alone on a mountain ridge, in a forest, or along a seashore is a needed aspect of personal well-being. Family life can also make personal demands that are relieved by being alone on a trail, which offers real healing and comfort. Nature is always there, twenty-four hours a day, ready to be experienced through hiking.

PROMOTING FAMILY TOGETHERNESS

One of the most beneficial gifts parents can give to their children is the gift of the outdoors, a love of nature, and the skill of hiking. By trekking through nature together, a parent and child have the opportunity to become closer, bond in an enjoyable way, while sharing an activity that both enjoy. Communication can more easily flow out of a learning activity that is fun for both parent and child. And hiking is a great way to ease the tensions of family life—a natural stress reducer. Living in a crowded home can test even the best relationships. Why not escape into the great outdoors together?

Hiking is noncompetitive; the one who wins when taking a hike is the individual who has gained from all the benefits that hiking offers. For families, hiking enhances and strengthens family relationships. When parents start hiking with their children early on (when kids are five or six years old), they encourage them to develop a lifelong interest and enthusiasm for the outdoors.

Hiking, out in nature, is free from the interruptions found in the home. No telephones, doorbells, or neighbors are there to distract the family tranquillity. Fathers and mothers can freely share with each other the delights discovered along the trail. The children are relieved from being parented in a disciplinary way, told what to do, and the parents likewise are freed from having to overly direct their children—especially if parents guide their children to safe and proper trail etiquette from their first hiking experiences. For some useful tips on hiking with kids, whether infants or teens, check out *Kids in the Wild* by Cindy Ross and Todd Gladfelter (The Mountaineers, 1995), a family guide to outdoor recreation.

There is a natural flow during a hike, where children come upon animals, plants, and other surprises and turn to parents more as co-hiking friends, asking them what the significance of this-or-that is and whether the parents will join them in exploring a meadow, a rock outcropping, a patch of wildflowers, etc. Parents and children develop a bond with each other as playful friends, co-explorers, and mutual nature enthusiasts. Indeed, as children reach the ages of eight or ten, they are able to accompany parents on much longer hikes, begin expanding their own growing physical energy, and provide a truer sense of being hiking companions to their parents.

In a very positive and bonding manner, each parent might hike with a certain child for the sole purpose of sharing important life information, of getting to honestly know a child as a person in their own right. A mother might grow closer to a daughter, a father to his son, as they adventure through nature—together. Hiking provides a much freer and less structured setting, where both parent and children have left the everyday stresses, identities, and roles back home. New personal expressions of challenging themselves, finding new interests in the natural world, learning the power of silence and tranquil beauty—all combine to encourage each adult parent and child to redefine themselves, share this newfound self with each other, and begin appreciating the uniqueness that each person expresses.

Fathers can discover their daughters, mothers their sons; if a single parent hikes, they can enjoy this same voyage of discovery with their children and might also consider inviting an adult family friend, so that at certain times during the hike, they might be alone with one of their children.

Hiking with Kids
In planning your hike, accommodate the needs of the least experienced and conditioned child, especially if you are in a mixed group of children of varying ages. If there are enough adults along, you can split the group into an older and more conditioned group. However you do it, children should always be with the group and not be allowed to leave the trail, staying within eyesight at all times. Appoint a leader and a trail "sweep," someone who will make sure that all hikers are on the trail in front of the sweep.

If you must discipline your children, take them aside rather than embarrassing them in front of their friends. Be ready to deal with the changing moods of your children. What was fun and exciting one week might become a boring drag the next. Patience is required, along with a plan to deal with situations that might arise. It's a good idea for both parents to talk over their game plan in dealing with what might come up, so that they present a united and decisive front to their children. The last thing your kids need is a set of arguing parents in the midst of nature's splendor.

Take the same snacking foods that your children usually enjoy, although offering them the option of creating their own trail mix can be quite fun. Check their pack before leaving! Make sure that they have brought enough water, the right clothes, and healthy food. Once on the trail, it is quite discouraging to discover that they "forgot" to bring water, or left their fruit and snacks on the kitchen table.

The Outdoor Classroom
Nature is a ready-made classroom. Plant and animal life make for great lessons in botany and biology. Having kids identify plants and animals can turn a hike into a fun game; bird-watching, rock collecting, even fossil discoveries lead to lessons in geology, earth history, geography, etc. During a hike, students can learn the basics of weather, topography, erosion, and even astronomy. Map reading is a skill kids find an easy connection with; at any given section of a trail, pull out your topo map and have someone in the group interpret how the immediate surroundings are reflected on the map. Make a game of it by having students predict what land features lie ahead.

Younger children can collect leaves, learn the difference between various kinds of trees, or discover the effects of running water as a force of erosion. All students can begin to understand how nature is so interconnected, and how ecosystems are populated and function, and how the seasons affect change in a given environment. After a hike through nature, visiting the library and reading together is a natural followup activity. The outdoor classroom piques the students' interest in what they've seen.

Building Self-Esteem and Confidence
Teens enjoy being with adults when both can let their hair down, drop their roles and relate person-to-person. Youth needs to be challenged and structured with a healthy discipline. Teens especially have energy to burn. Hiking gives them an ideal outlet for exercise, entertaining themselves, and building relationships with other peers, friends, and family. Hiking alone also shows them a way in which they can take time out from life's distractions, reflect on critical decisions they might be pondering in their life—thus learning to evaluate and not react to what life throws their way. The encouragement that hiking gives someone while wandering through nature, absorbing inspirations, lessons, and strength, serves youth through a lifetime of trials and tribulations.

Outdoor survival schools might just be the challenge your teens are looking for or need. These schools focus on teaching not only hiking skills, but backpacking, mountaineering, rock climbing, camping, and outdoor survival. There are organizations, such as some YMCA groups, that sponsor survival camps at various national parks or even state parks. The scouting programs for both young men and women also specialize in introducing youth to outdoor skills. Some of these training programs include winter and water survival, up to two-week backpacks, and other challenges that serve to build self-confidence. Check the magazine advertisements in the back of outdoor magazines, as well as local YMCA/YWCA groups.

Teens are very prone to exploring and discovering the larger world after leaving school. Hiking offers them an entry into the wild lands of the United States. Having learned the skills and pleasures of hiking when young, they can begin uncovering all of nature's treasures for themselves. If they attend college, hiking, camping or backpacking trips are a great way to socialize or get the proper exercise to support all those mental pursuits.

Years later, children will fondly remember special days on the trail, the time they first climbed a mountain, came across spectacular mountain meadows filled with rainbows of wildflowers, tested themselves in some desert canyon, came over a ridge to discover the expanses of the valley below, saw their first eagle, deer, or elk—and in gratitude they will share these same gifts with their children, inviting the grandparents of their children along to share the magic once shared with them.

ROMANCE ON THE TRAIL

Building Personal Connections

"A joy shared is a joy doubled."

—*Goethe*

Most hikers have a special fondness for a particular trail—a meandering path along a cool stream, a sandy landscape surrounded by huge boulders, or a foot path that leads into a forest of evergreen trees thick enough to block out the sun. We foster a communion with remote areas like these, coming back time and time again just to be in our favorite place. While many may prefer to visit such special places alone, others can find great joy by sharing the experience, the closeness to nature and solitude, with someone special.

Couples who hike create emotional ties with each other. In the intimate privacy of the outdoors, people can communicate freely, without distractions and noise from the outside world. It is this bond that strengthens relationships and teaches us how to appreciate each other.

SELF-HELP BOOKS THAT DON'T HELP

How to be a better lover. How to sexually satisfy your mate. How to tell your significant other how you really feel without hurting his/her feelings. We've heard about these self-help books on radio and television talk shows. Maybe we've even read a few. But did they really help? Did they really give you tools to understand the one you love? Maybe it's time to let nature inspire you.

Gather a group of hikers for a fireside chat, and you'll most likely hear testimony about external versus internal backpacks, the best sleeping bag on the market, or rough-and-tumble trails up the side of a cliff. Chances are nobody would dare bring up the subject of romance. But, admit it or not, romance exists on the trail.

There are times when nature stirs our hearts and makes us loving. Many couples have said they enjoy one another especially during a hike. Walking through nature can be one of the most uplifting and bonding experiences two people can share. It's invigorating to the mind and spirit. Senses such as sight, smell, and touch come alive. Mountains, flowers, trees, creeks, wildlife—all burst onto the scene with tremendous vitality. Your body is energized by inhaling the pure, clean, fresh air. Each breath makes you stronger. You want to climb, romp around, hold hands. You are in the middle of an explosion of beauty and energy. And right there, through it all, walking next to you, is the one you love.

Hiking takes couples into perfect romantic settings that enhance the physical and spiritual side of a relationship: quiet lakes, meadows of wild flowers, a brilliant full-moon desert landscape, or a spectacular vista from atop a canyon wall. It allows people to talk to each other and reveal what's on their minds and what's inside their hearts. And this kind of sharing connects hearts and souls through the shared joy of the outdoors.

LOVE OUTDOOR STYLE

Here's a tale of true romance:

It was a great day to read a thriller or mystery under a plush duvet or wrapped in a fuzzy bathrobe. It was the type of cold and rainy day perfect for baking cookies or writing letters to friends. It was the kind of day to do anything but venture outside. Anyone with an ounce of logic would have stayed home inside, warm and dry.

The local television forecaster said if you had to go outside, bundle up, break out the umbrella and rain coat. Although it was the first day of a three-day holiday weekend, most people would have followed the forecaster's sound advice and stayed put. Most—but not everyone.

A certain young couple decided it was the perfect time to get out of town. Craving a hike, they drove two hours outside of Palm Springs, California, to an isolated area of Anza Borrego State Park. They'd been there countless times before. They had heard about a delightful trail up a quaint stream into an oasis of palm trees, just the perfect respite they were seeking. Nearby was a beautiful old resort— unknown to all but faithful followers who had visited it since the early '60s without telling their friends and family. Too many visitors would spoil its charm.

The pair were unprepared for a hike in wet weather. Wearing shorts, baseball caps, and hiking boots, they sloshed up the trail along the rushing stream, its waters gurgling from the heavy downpour the night before. Although others chose to heed the weather forecaster's warning, these two wanted to play outside, get wet, and be kids again.

The couple headed up Palm Canyon Trail, an easy 2-mile walk into the hills of the state park. Ash-colored storm clouds hovered above the hilltops. Rain was coming, no doubt about that. The clouds cast an eerie, almost wicked shadow across the stream. On the ground, fallen palm fronds saturated with rain covered the trail.

Just another perfect rainy day in the desert, and these two adventurers were reveling in it. Sure, a warm, sunny day would have been great, but when you're with someone you like a lot, or are deeply in love with, hiking can bring you closer together.

After walking the Palm Canyon Trail in Anza Borrego, the young couple in love went to their favorite hidden resort, took a long, relaxing bubble bath, enjoyed a delicious nap holding each other, and woke up feeling refreshed, rejuvenated, and loved.

MAKING TIME FOR EACH OTHER BY HIKING

As the demands of our daily lives—jobs, household bills, mortgages or rent, car payments, children, in-laws—limit our free time, couples have to really struggle, schedule, and set aside quality time for each other. All too often there aren't enough hours in the day to do that.

And when night time arrives, most couples simply don't have the energy or strength to talk, cuddle, or just hold each other. After a full day at work, cleaning up after dinner, reading to your children (if you have any), throwing a small load into the laundry, and watching the evening news, how romantic do you feel?

A mother of two small children said that before she married, she loved to plan picnics with her then-boyfriend, spend time reading to each other, and laying out by a pool. Simple, inexpensive pleasures brought them closer together. Then the two married. Their world changed. Gone were the picnics, reading sessions, and poolside chats. Gone was the sense of playfulness that the two enjoyed during their courtship.

When children entered the picture, romance took a back seat. Both worked and raised the children. Both loved each other and the family, and both said they didn't have time to think about making time for each other. I'm not a therapist or expert on marriage by any stretch of the imagination. But I do know that couples need time to be with one another.

Partners are often faced with little time to talk, share experiences, or hug and kiss. Although it takes time, planning, and some preparation, hiking can bring two people closer together, help them love each other more, and bring out the best qualities that too often get buried by the hectic demands of daily life. On the trail, the telephone stops ringing, the kids are not there to make demands on you, you are both free from the roles and identity of career . . . free to be more yourselves and to see each other in a gentler, kinder light.

Alone, in nature, couples can renew their love for each other, rediscover their partner and friend, build a long "life history" of shared adventures and hikes spent together on the trail. The key to building this positive shared intimacy is for each partner to drop what roles define them in the relationship and approach being together as two friends, open to each other's needs while responding to each person's uniqueness.

I suggest that couples literally "stay together" while hiking, and avoid having one partner race ahead because she or he is stronger or in better shape. Hiking is not a contest; if a person feels the need for an "exercise"-focused hike, where the object is to burn calories big-time and cover longer distances than one's partner is up for—then hike alone or with a friend who is into that kind of hike. There is so much more joy in "being together," sharing personal feelings, concerns, dreams, and enthusiasms found in nature; you can't develop this aspect of intimacy miles apart on a trail! Besides, if you find yourself especially moved by what you experience along the way, you'll want to turn to that special someone and give them a warm hug and a passionate kiss of joy!

Take Roger and Maria Keezer, the couple in their sixties who we met in chapter 5, The Physical Benefits of Hiking. The Keezers love to hike and spend time outside together. In the beginning it was a little difficult for Maria to keep up with her husband. But, with time, she has increased her pace while he has slowed to accommodate her. She has become a regular traveler who loves the wilderness because it clears her mind while she shares the experience with her husband.

HIKING BRINGS US CLOSER TOGETHER

But enough of this mushy stuff about romantic walks and staring into each other's eyes as you munch trail mix. Any devoted outdoor lover—or lover of the wilderness—knows there's something about being in the wilds that turns us on, brings out the wild animal in some. What is it? The crisp morning air nibbles at your ears, the cool breeze caresses your hair, the scent of pine moves you to feel something. Outdoorspeople call it a love of nature, being free, celebrating who you really are. When you walk outside—into the mountains, valleys, or forests—the soul is stirred. It's as though some incredible force—God, a Native American Great Spirit, the universal energy—touches you and you become energized. Some react to that love of nature by bestowing love onto another person . . . your hiking companion.

Only you can define how you love someone. But when you're at peace, stress-free, feeling good, you may want to share it with someone. Hiking can fulfill this desire to share good times with another.

The beauty of the wilderness piques your sense of spirituality. Do you remember a tear forming in your eye when you saw the most amazing natural wonder in nature?—a tremendous waterfall, a glowing sunrise, a high-rising plateau, or the first fall of snow in the middle of a pine forest. It's these images and memories that help us forget we are employees, bread winners, corporate junkies, and help us remember we are human. And all humans need love.

When we hike and share the experience with another—a friend, a relative, a partner, a lover—we receive more than we give. Sharing intensifies our own inner experiences. Hiking with a buddy, a lover, a spouse, brings back those feelings of fulfillment, companionship.

Remember the first time you and your significant other saw a sunset? What was it like? Can you recall the feelings you had for the other person at that time? Didn't your soul fill with love for the person sitting beside you? Didn't you wish this feeling would never go away?

It doesn't have to. If you rekindle and strengthen the love you have for someone every time you take a hike together, chances are the bonding love will last.

Hiking gives us a perspective on ourselves and our lives, on what matters and what has value. Hiking with a companion helps both people appreciate each other, as we see the value that the other person has in our lives. If fulfillment comes more from sharing love and having someone there to receive it, then during our most intense, uplifting moments on the trail, all we need do is to quietly turn to the person next to us and recognize the role he or she plays in our fulfillment . . . our companion has given us the opportunity to be our loving self with them . . . our very best self.

Don't relationship counselors tell us to share our feelings and thoughts with others? Isn't open and honest communication the key to every successful relationship? Why don't more couples venture outside and spend time surrounded by nature? Rather than screaming and hollering at each other, try listening quietly to the wind as it sweeps through a canyon. Share what it means to be a hiker with someone you love. Hikers are genuinely open to new experiences, different challenges, new paths. If you have never been on a trail in your life, give it try with a close friend or lover. The new experience will draw you closer to each other if you are compatible. It can be exciting and fun to explore new places. Couples who hike together cannot help but feel love toward each other.

One memorable sunset I vividly recall was high above the Amazon rain forest in Peru. My boyfriend and I climbed up a canopy built by botanists and scientists to study plant and animal life several hundred feet above the jungle floor. We saw an ocean of green treetops so thick you could imagine walking across them and never touching the jungle floor. We sat and waited until the edge of the green foliage sea swallowed a pinkish-red sun. In the distant, the screech of jungle monkeys and parakeets echoed one last time before retiring for the night. Chirping crickets and the buzz of night beetles filled the air. The sun slowly dropped down to the other side of the world. And after all the beautiful pink, orange, and yellow rays of the sun, darkness; we sat and watched in awe. We smiled, gave each other a tender kiss and began the descent to the jungle floor.

Another couple I know promised to love each other forever high atop a mountain. They had been dating for several years and knew they had found a soulmate in each other. Both loved the outdoors. At the end of a hike to a mountaintop, they rested, sipped cool water, and quietly observed the world around them. The glorious sun was about to set. A breeze softly tousled their hair. It was a special moment. After a long pause for solace, he rummaged through his backpack pretending to look for a bite to eat. She continued to watch the impressive view, pine trees everywhere. She felt so happy to be here with her boyfriend, her companion. He presented a ring to her and asked for her hand in marriage. The two married a year later and have hiked up that same trail again and again.

RENEWING YOUR LOVING SELF
BY HIKING WITH FRIENDS

I know of several women who enjoy hiking with each other—leaving their husbands or boyfriends at home. All say they like the time away from their mates to learn how to truly love and appreciate them. "My husband is not as strong a hiker as I am," said one woman. "We love hiking the gentle trails together, but when I want a tough, strenuous hike, I call one of my girlfriends."

On the way home after a hike with her friend, this woman says she looks forward to seeing her husband, to tell him about her day. "I already feel great when I come down that mountain. My spirits are high, my energy level is high. It's a wonderful feeling to share that with him."

Besides the emotions created during a hike, energy is generated, energy that supports an open enthusiasm toward one's partner, as well as the openness to be and share yourself. This energy can take a lover's expression through sexuality; it can also be an open flow of communication, or the subtle but strong bonds of togetherness. Whatever form it takes, it is infused with the same love that nature inspires in us during every step along the trail.

HIKING AND CREATIVITY

Finding Inspiration
in Nature

*"The sight of anything extremely beautiful, in nature or
in art, brings back the memory of what one loves, with
the speed of lightning. That is, . . . all that is beautiful
and sublime in the world takes part in the beauty of what
one loves, and this unexpected glimpse of happiness
immediately fills the eyes with tears. This is how love
of the beautiful and love give each other life."*

—*Stendhal,* De l'amour

If we listen carefully, nature will speak to us—in the stillness of a surrounding forest, the call of a bird far away,
the wind streaming through the trees, or the noise of a
rushing river. If we listen, we are calm and receptive to
what nature has to say. In this calmness, we feel nature's
words through our hearts and minds.

In his book *The Celestine Prophecy,* James Redfield describes a spiritual exploration, with key insights all aimed
at moving humankind closer to nature, strengthening our

bond with the earth, and helping us find inner peace and clarity. It is a guide for listening to nature.

"Looking at the distant mountains, I noticed that a daytime moon had been out and was about to set. It looked to be about a quarter full and hung over the horizon like an inverted bowl. Instantly I understood why it had that shape. The sun, millions of miles directly above me, was shining only on top of the sinking moon. I could perceive the exact line between the sun and the lunar surface, and this recognition somehow extended my consciousness outward even farther," Redfield writes.

Redfield preaches about getting back to nature. For centuries humans have had a fascination with the outdoors. Whether it was an attempt to conquer and control it, or a curious journey to learn more, the fascination always endured.

You've read about the physical benefits of hiking in chapter 5, how it can cleanse your mind and ability to think clearer and how it can help you build confidence. There are those who need to explore the wilderness in order to make sense of the world around them. There are people who hike, walk, and explore the land to remember that humans are just visitors on planet Earth. We are responsible for taking care of it, its creatures, and each other. In return, Earth gives us spiritual rebirth, inner peace, joy, fresh air, and, if we choose to accept, a healthy lifestyle.

In addition, the colors, forms, and textures found only in forests, deserts, rivers, valleys, or mountains are the elements that creative people use to make their handiwork. You must be willing to be inspired by nature. These elements offer new material for the artist.

HIKING NURTURES THE ARTIST

Fabric designer Erica Hopper of Rancho Mirage, California, seeks inspiration from the texture, colors, and designs she observes from her weekly hikes into the Santa Rosa Mountains near her home. "Hiking is certainly a positive for most ailments, mental and physical. It is a soother of the soul, abstains pain, clarifies thought, empties out the garbage, opens avenues of adventure, health awareness, confidence, and simply appreciation," she said.

Imagination is a gift for an artist. It allows Hopper to paint and design wonderful stories on canvas. But for many artists, sometimes the inspiration is lacking and the creative juices fail to flow. "There are moments of course while implementing my ideas on canvas that indecision pops up out of nowhere. I'm baffled with one particular concept or color meshing. I am blocked for some reason and it's now time to break away for some new silence and surroundings."

Hiking allows her to focus on her creativity. The wilderness, the pumping adrenaline, a trust of the unknown all broaden her sense of direction, sharpen her perceptions and her application of color, erase the frustration, and clarify the confusion, helping her find a solution.

Hopper began hiking in earnest and has fallen in love with this pastime, so in love that she and her husband have traveled to Zion National Park in Utah, to Wyoming, and to other spectacular outdoor settings for creative inspiration. "The visual stimulation has been incredible: sandstone, plant life, magnificent vistas, and geological formations all yield fantastic textures, graphic possibilities, and new ways of interpreting the way that color, form, and shape come together artistically," she said about hiking.

THE ARTIST RECIPROCATES

How do we know nature truly inspires us? What goes on in the minds of creative people who hike? Have you ever stood in awe before a photo by Ansel Adams of Yosemite National Park and wondered, "How did he do that?" It seems as though Adams was able to capture the feeling of the scene.

Whether it be a photo of the brave face of Half Dome or a quiet meadow, nature seems to be communicating with us. But what does it say? What was it about that particular scene that attracted the photographer, sketch artist, or painter to pause? What did the person feel at that moment? What do we feel as observers? Love for nature and a responsibility to care for it? These questions drive creative people to walk in the hills, mountains, forests, or deserts to explore the answers. They are hungry for inspiration and creativity. They need a spiritual force to tap into and give them the mental and imaginative tools to write, paint, sketch, design.

Wildlife and nature photographers love the adventure of an assignment. Many go to feel a part of the natural land and animals they choose to photograph. "It's a peaceful feeling to see a mother bear and her little cubs wrestle in a green meadow," said one photographer. "All of a sudden, I know what I have to do. They are the inspiration I need to do my job."

Fortunately, cameras have the ability to freeze an inspirational moment so that others can enjoy it later. Creators of art, paintings, poetry, fiction, and nonfiction are constantly seeking inspiration. It doesn't come in a jar, cannot be bought in a drugstore, and will never grow on trees. Some artists, writers, and philosophers need to go outside to become inspired for their work.

Many artists are self-appointed conservationists who see it as their job to defend the wilderness with a camera, a sketch, or words. The pictures and images they create are meant to inspire others to save the natural lands, conserve the virgin forests, and above all, treasure all the creatures who live in the natural world.

HIKING UNBLOCKS OUR CREATIVITY

If you write, you are familiar with writer's block. It's frustrating, time-consuming, and downright painful. The flesh is willing but the spirit is weak, right? You're all ready to go, sitting in front of a computer, typewriter, or notepad, and . . . nothing. The mind goes blank. It happens all too often.

When I experience writer's block, I usually take a break, go for a walk, sit outside, and look at the mountains nearby or stretch. If I am able, I take a short hike by my apartment up a small face of a mountain. I particularly like this little jaunt when the sun is about to set and a cool breeze is blowing in the air. It's a short drive to get there but the mental awareness, refreshment, and inspiration I get on that hike is worth it. The breeze caresses my face, the sun feels good on my back, and the wall that blocked my creativity before is slowly fading away. Hiking provides a stimulating and energizing environment.

I can remember a fellow hiker I met a few years ago on a trail in Sedona, Arizona. He was sitting on a flat rock, hunched over, busy with his hands. As I walked past him, he looked up to say hello. He was typing on a laptop computer! Extraordinary, I thought. Curious, I asked him what he was writing. Surely nothing can be so important that a laptop must be hauled in a backpack up a trail. It was. As it turned out, he was writing a love letter to his girlfriend who couldn't be with him during this trip. "The best way to tell her what I see is to look at it as I write," he said. Colorful description of the canyon below, the trees swaying back and forth in the wind, and the outstretched rays of a setting sun would be lost if he wrote the letter after the hike. He called the experience very rewarding, almost spiritual. "It's like having her here beside me," I remember him saying.

ONENESS WITH NATURE

Nature lover and writer Henry David Thoreau wrote, "You cannot perceive beauty but with a serene mind." So we head out into nature to find our serene mind. But because our world is busy, fast-paced, stressful, and hectic, it is difficult to find serenity. For some of us, our minds are so programmed to talk, analyze, evaluate, judge, or predict, we can't turn them off. When we go for a walk, the beauty of nature helps turn the mind chatter off and encourages us to witness what is happening around us. Our senses absorb the environment.

Artists are able to do this. In their reflective and sensitive mode, they are able to pick out details, notice colors, and achieve happiness in their hearts. It will take practice if you've never done this before. But don't give up. It will happen.

Hiking allows us to explore points of views and frames of reference that we normally wouldn't think about in our lives if we didn't walk with nature. The interaction between a person and a waterfall, mist over a lake, an oddly shaped tree, or a majestic cliff allows us to be more creative. The images Adams and other naturalists and photographers captured are not only pictures on film. They are moods, attitudes, a way of honoring the land.

Textile artist and painter Margaret Moran said she has reached an inner balance in her life, a point where she understands and likes herself. She paints, designs fabrics, and writes poetry from her studio and home in Portland, Oregon. "I've reached this level and it's so refreshing. I am able to think clearer and focus on my work," she said. Moran receives her inspiration from the "muse," a creative force that comes to her unannounced. She has achieved this sensitive level through deep meditation and balance in her life, which includes long walks in nature with her friends. A lifelong student of philosophy, psychology, and metaphysics, Moran enjoys the oneness with nature and herself. "I love being among the trees. They are so beautiful to look at. I love feeling free." This freedom of creative exploration allows Moran to do her work without expectations or judgment from others, to express herself without fearing what others will say about her or her work.

Does the earth speak to select individuals only? What can we learn about ourselves, our talents, and our world if we open our hearts and minds? Native people often can pick up messages from the land. Society at large feels a weakened relationship with the earth. For many of us the connection doesn't exist.

Native Americans, however, have "a respect for the earth that comes from a genuine feeling of being part of it. The land is who they are, that's the way they express it, and every part of it is precious," said Peter Matthiessen in Jonathan White's book *Talking on the Water: Conversations About Nature.* In several indigenous cultures, people have a sense of connection with the land. Everything is sacred. The Western sense of being part of the land would be labeled as environmentalism, Matthiessen says. We will never experience the land as these Native people did. These true believers of the power of nature became one with the earth in all its glory. Humans are made from the earth. Inspiration to live better, healthier, and stronger exists if we only make the conscious effort to be open to the inspirations of nature.

SEEING NATURE WITH NEW EYES

Albert Einstein once observed that he discovered the theory of relativity because he was free to think in the job he held at the Swiss Patent Office; more importantly, he had retained his childlike ability to see the world simply and ask the simple questions of a child. Hiking takes us into nature and supports our leaving behind old world views. We momentarily exit our paradigm—the roles, attitudes, perceptions, and expectations that mold and sometimes limit us in our daily routine. On the trail we are unburdened by these mental constructs. In this state, people can see what nature offers in order to inspire fresh insights for problem solving, writing, and artistic expressions using color, form, texture, and shape.

Beethoven frequented the countryside around Vienna and the famed Vienna Woods for gaining new musical inspirations. The Hopi, Navaho, and many other Indian tribes have expressed the impact of nature in their artistic creations of jewelry, sand paintings, bead and basket weaving, totem carving, and much more. Nature inspired the transcendentalists of New England and the Romantic poets like Keats, Shelley, Wordsworth, Byron, and others. Culture has always been influenced by the natural setting the artist and thinker found themselves in.

But people dealing with the everyday can also, by experiencing nature, discover creative inspirations. Business problems and life concerns can all be successfully addressed by the creative problem solving inspired by nature. Nature offers us the opportunity, through solitude, to look inward and find solutions in the creative wellspring of our own selves. And if all art is imitation, to some degree, at least in nature we find subject matter worthy of imitation.

THE SPIRITUALITY OF HIKING

A Prayer
in Motion

"The beauty of the trees, the softness of the air,
The fragrance of the grass, speaks to me.
The summit of the mountain, the thunder of the sky,
The rhythm of the sea, speaks to me.
The faintness of the stars, the freshness of the morning,
The dewdrop on the flower, speaks to me.
The strength of fire, the taste of salmon,
The trail of the sun, and the life that never goes away,
They speak to me. And my heart soars."

—*Chief Dan George*

A theologian from my university once remarked to me that the first commandment, "I am the Lord thy God, thou shalt not have strange gods before me," was meant to reach far beyond the ancient custom of worshipping idols of stone or gold. It was an admonition that nothing should ever come between humans and God, nothing in human nature should dominate the human heart and psyche, drive us to action, more than our relationship to God. And whenever we allowed a false imbalance to take place, we would feel it in the form of suffering, even before we might be aware that we had "sinned."

Over the centuries we've created products of civilization that draw us away from ourselves. Technology gives us access to the media, television, radio, computers, and now the Internet. We live our lives reacting to what we see and hear, distracted by entertainment, information, things to buy, and the many other noises of the modern world...all of a human origin. In being drawn away from ourselves, we are also pulled away from God and our spiritual center, if one believes that the kingdom of God is within. Daily life provides us with a multitude of "idols" vying for our attention. The irony is that if the polls are correct, that many of us simply do not trust either our institutions or each other, then why do we pursue these creations, these false idols?

Yet it wasn't always this way. Humans have, from our earliest beginnings, recognized a divine presence in nature. Our ancestors worshipped forces of fire, wind, trees, water, the sun, etc., as manifestations of divine power. In the Hebrew tradition of both the Old and the New Testament, prophets, kings, holy men, and the Christ went out into nature to meditate. Spending time in the wilderness to pray was, for Jesus, an act of worship, a time set aside to connect with his heavenly father, to stand in the divine presence and gain peace of mind, love of heart, and guidance in life.

American Indians are a people especially aware of the Great Spirit found in nature. The sun, wind, trees, mountains, and animals manifested God, while nature provided the best place where the Great Spirit could be experienced. Thus many an Indian slipped away to offer prayers upon high, windswept mesas, in quiet lakeside settings, and in the open expanses of almost infinite desert or prairie.

Hiking provides us with a pathway into nature, which offers us a quiet, "free-from-idols" place to connect with God, whatever we know and experience this divine presence to be. Chapter 4, Stress Management and Hiking, emphasized the emptying effects of hiking—our minds are cleared, our emotions are settled, stress, worldly concerns, and problems fall away. We are left open and ready for any inspiration and spiritual experience that might be offered us. Prayer comes more easily. In nature, during a hike, we find sanctuary.

THE BLESSINGS OF BEING IN NATURE

"Grant me the ability to be alone; May it be my custom to go outdoors each day among the trees and grasses, among all growing things and there may I be alone, and enter into prayer to talk with the one that I belong to."
—*Rabbi Nachman of Bratzlav*

Once we've taken ourselves into nature, it is up to the individual to communicate with God in the way he or she is most comfortable. For some this means silent listening.

Nature is a perfect place for this quiet experience. I've found myself on plateaus looking out into the distant expanses of a Utah desert, a sea of pinkish red, greens, beige, and lilac rock and sand. The stillness is uplifting, the divine presence real. Nature, with its special traits of power, beauty, grace, and infinity, mirrors the soul of the creator within and behind his creation. In those very special places known only to a hiker who has made the effort to reach them, God welcomes the journeyer with blessings of peace, joy, love, and an embrace only the wilderness can give. For we are physical, flesh and blood, and often our hearts are first touched by the passionate excitement of the senses fulfilled by scents, wind, sun, water, and physical textures of plant life, rock, and soil—nature's personality.

But there is also another blessing that nature bestows on its visitors: energy. What is the effect on someone paging through a picture book of nature photography that brilliantly captures the combination of nature's most vibrant colors and inspirational scenes? That person feels uplifted, positive, and energized. He or she might even exude passion and admiration for the emotional power of those pictures. Nature has been captured at her best, frame after frame of inspiring scenes.

But how much more powerfully energizing are the effects of actually "being in those pictures" by hiking to those places? Our eyes are awed at every turn, for with every glance in any direction nature offers us a "framed picture" like walking through a museum, examining each individual photograph while drawing aesthetic energy from everything we see.

Part of this energy is surely the silent realization that our souls and hearts are being fed with the very love that the creator put into every scene, and used to fashion the entire fabric of nature. A. R. Orage asserts that "love is for creation . . . that it always creates." Nature bears this imprint of love throughout its diversity. The psalmist in Psalm 103 (13:30) cries out that "the earth is filled with the fruit of Thy works . . . when Thou sendest forth Thy spirit, they are created, and Thou renewest the face of the earth."

Redfield's *The Celestine Prophecy* suggested that some-day humans would live "in the most powerful and beautiful places on earth," i.e., nature, especially in and around trees. Great and meaningful intuitions would come to those who entered into nature's bounty, be it on forest paths or traveling through sacred canyons. According to Redfield, people would finally "grasp how beautiful and spiritual the natural world really is. We'll see trees and rivers and mountains as temples of great power to be held in reverence and awe"—something that American Indians and the psalmists of the Old Testament already had direct experience with and testimony about.

Thus uplifted in spirit, hiking prepares us for the journey within ourselves and for the encounter with God as revealed to any open and seeking heart. The psalmists experienced this divine presence in nature, and encouraged people to seek God there.

NATURE SPIRITUALLY TRANSFORMS US

"The heavens declare the glory of God, and the firmament proclaims the work of His hands. Day declares the message unto day, and night unto night reveals this knowledge. There is neither speech nor discourse, their voice cannot be heard."
—*Psalm 18:1, 2*

What happens in nature, as we make our way through the silent mountains, the still forest, the expanse of prairie or the wild, far-reaching canyons and deserts? With each step we shed a bit of "the world," our identities in it, our attachments and concerns. By so doing, we begin to approach what it means to be spiritual—of the spirit and nothing else. Freed from desire and expectation, as hiking brings us into the cathedral of land, sky, and the natural world, we prepare ourselves for knowing and being known, for waiting to be touched by the God present in his works.

The great Jewish philosopher Martin Buber wrote in *I and Thou* that "All real living is meeting. The relationship to the *Thou* is direct. No system of ideas, no foreknowledge, and no fancy intervene between *I* and *Thou*. The memory itself is transformed, as it plunges out of its isolation into the unity of the whole. No aim, no lust, and no anticipation intervene between *I* and *Thou*. Desire itself is transformed as it plunges out of its dream into the appearance. Every means is an obstacle. Only when every means has collapsed does the meeting come about."

God, the divine presence in nature, is this "Thou" to which Buber refers. By going out into nature and being emptied by its influence, our true and real *I* or self can stand in relationship to God, our *Thou*. Hiking into nature helps this process by offering us a desire-free, idea-free, means-free environment. We cannot "use" the nature we encounter on a hike or think it to be anything other than what it simply presents itself as being. We are left standing alone, as is, to begin the process of turning to meet God, leaving all other worldly concerns and considerations behind. We meet God. Our *I* meets the *Thou* of his being, much like when two lovers exist in the present moment, side by side, saying nothing, thinking nothing—just being with each other. This is central to being spiritual, and having no other idols before us to distract us from being with the divine presence.

Famous naturalist John Muir was described by biographer Edwin Teale as "intensely religious. The forests and the mountains formed his temple. His approach to all nature was worshipful. He saw everything evolving yet everything the direct handiwork of God. There was a spiritual and religious exaltation in his experiences with nature. And he came down from the mountains like some bearded prophet to preach of the beauty and healing he had found in this natural temple where he worshipped." Perhaps no one except Henry Thoreau "had so pure and lofty a vision of man's ultimate relationship to nature."

A JOURNEY INTO NATURE

"When we get out of the glass bottles of our ego,
and when we escape like squirrels turning in the cages
of our personality
and get into the forests again, we shall shiver with
cold and fright
but things will happen to us so that we don't know
ourselves.
Cool, unlying life will rush in,
and passion will make our bodies taut with power,
we shall stamp our feet with new power and old
things will fall down,
we shall laugh, and institutions will curl up like burnt
paper."
—D. H. Lawrence, The Plumed Serpent

One summer I journeyed up into the high mountains west of Denver for my own spiritual encounter with nature. In just minutes I found myself at 7,500 feet, surrounded by the higher foothills of the Rocky Mountains. No sign of human habitat could be seen, save for the road that got me there. It still amazes me that my summer home rests on the far western edge of the plains where the prairie, beginning 1,000 miles east in Ohio and sweeping across Indiana, Illinois, Missouri, Kansas, and parts of Colorado, abruptly stops. The great wall of the Rocky Mountains thrusts up, seemingly out of nowhere, to claim the land and shadow the endless eastern plains with its majestic presence.

Leaving my vehicle, I stepped onto the trail and began winding my way westward. The early summer rains had done their work. Spread in all directions and tucking itself into and under the canopy of ponderosa pine, fir, spruce, and aspen was an intensely green carpet of prairie grasses, three feet high in some places. Sprinkled generously throughout this green carpet were thousands of wildflowers, blue and purple lupine, asters, wild rose, yellow gaillardia, sulfur flowers, red and orange Indian paintbrush, and dozens of other species. The grasses were soft, forming waves of flowing green oceans that invited me in to touch the shimmering crests, while smelling their floral accents.

Spreading out near the trail were the many varieties of trees, some with leaves shimmering in the late afternoon breeze, quaking aspen and elm, but mostly with the pine needles of the mountain forests. The scent was especially strong, as it had rained for three days prior, and now the warm sun drew the rich, heavy odor of pine from the stately ponderosa and fir, mingled it with sweet prairie grass and the intoxicating perfumes of a thousand floral bouquets and overwhelmed me with this ambrosia of delight.

At first the trees stood singly away from the trail, some solitary or in pairs rooted in the rich earth and exulting in the azure Colorado sky, with extended families of six to a dozen behind them, dispersed throughout the grassy sea. An endless forest of dark green spread like a blanket over the nearby and distant mountain ridges, which stood row after row, ascending ever higher until reaching the snow-drenched peaks of the Continental Divide, the afternoon sun gleaming off their remaining snowfields like a sheet of brilliant white crystal. And all around me—stillness. Vibrant colors mingled with the soft strokes of an afternoon breeze, cool with the moisture left from the evening rains.

The land flowed away from the trail, forming valley after valley, as if washed down from the distant mountains, so expansive that I felt open to the endless sky and far horizons. From my vantage point I could see miles into the early summer evening, the sun still warm and only now beginning its descent toward the horizon. This was a region alive with the Colorado natural treasures that poets and naturalists, writers and outdoor adventurers had long admired.

I walked slowly that day. With a reverent pace, I absorbed the color, texture, and lay of the land, amazed at the landscaped design of the creator, so perfect in its balanced mix of trees, grass, flowers, mountains, and sky. Soon, some white cumulus clouds bubbled up, playing peek-a-boo with the surrounding mountain peaks, then boiling upward high enough to accent the sky, with their soft edges tinted in pink and blue shadows, promising a delightful sunset. The scene was complete. This was my "walking meditation," my journey into those spiritual realities I find in settings enriched by nature's abundant offerings.

The distant meadows, with their forest backdrops, drew me up the trail effortlessly. I was a prayer in motion, aware only of the natural treasures surrounding me, no thoughts, no concerns, just a memory of what I once felt long ago when, as a child, I explored nearby forests, free in spirit, enveloped in the caring protection of innocent childhood. So I had become "as a little child" again, as the Christ had instructed, playful, awed, without desire or need.

A quiet, deep joy arose in me. With each step, I took in the textured beauty and depth of the land and released back to it my heartfelt gratitude, joyful in the rebirth that was taking place. Isn't this the essence of spirituality, to be reborn in his image, a heart full of love, appreciating God's presence in his works? I approached some ponderosa pine and smelled its rich, warm, vanilla-scented bark, washed with rosy yellow light from the late afternoon sun, then knelt down in the surrounding meadows and with outstretched hands drew in bundles of wildflowers, drinking in their freshness.

Mile led to mile, time sifted away, evening drew near. Everywhere I felt the love of first the land, then the creator whose gift it was. When I finally turned around at trail's end, a feeling sprang up, conceived in the joy of the land. In partaking of each treasure this land offered, I wanted to thank someone for the goodness of nature's fulfillment. God was the presence I turned to with gratitude. My well-being now came from my relationship to the creator, a friendship I too often had stepped away from in the struggle and busy demands of my daily life.

While walking in this emptied state of mind, I became aware of simple spiritual truths that comforted me from the weary demands of a sometimes too cluttered lifestyle. By releasing all wanting, striving, or struggling during my hike, I had become open to a spiritual peace. No one in my life at that moment seemed a threat; nothing felt unfinished. Everything that should have been, was. I felt complete, regardless of what actions and decisions I might make in the future, or their outcome. I remembered the words of the Christian mystics, that in the loving presence of God, all is perfected.

The material goals I might have set for myself just hours before seemed less important. I was left feeling unattached to anything or any outcome. The simplicity of the present moment was enough.

I also felt closer to humanity. While passing another hiker, I imagined that the trail stretching before me was really the same trail we are all traveling. Being in nature is so unpretentious, free from status, the trappings of wealth or self-importance. Many a person in my hiking club spoke of this equalizing effect of hiking. Hikers became friends who would ordinarily never meet each other through the regular social channel of jobs and career.

I remembered a story from a philosophy lecture about an anthropologist touring a small South Sea island. He was accompanied by a Native guide. Whenever they met someone, the guide and strangers exchanged the same greeting. After the tour, the scientist observed what an incredibly friendly place this was. Everyone acted so civil toward each other. And what was that greeting that was so commonly shared? His guide replied that the closest translation for the greeting was "I am you." My hike that afternoon in Colorado emphasized that same reality to me. The oneness I felt with nature extended to all other human beings.

John Muir observed that healing is one of the spiritual benefits nature bestows upon its visitors. Part of that healing comes from the connection hikers experience not only with themselves but with nature and all life. This connectedness encourages a sense of belonging, which acts like a powerful agent to dispel loneliness and feelings of rejection. Being in nature solidifies the bonds we have with the human community and with the animal world. We feel our compassionate relationship with all beings, all living things . . . a child of the universe once again. No longer feeling separate, we return to the human experience with a renewed sense of belonging and acceptance.

I finished my hike that day with a silent meditation. Perching on a rock outcropping nestled in a small grove of pine, I gazed out into the prairie, through the opening of Eldorado Canyon. Lying directly on the plain in front of me was Denver, shimmering like some half-dream that found itself out of place in the comforting natural realities surrounding me. And yet, after any sojourn in the wilderness, every hike ends by turning homeward. Nature had spiritualized my humanity, not only on the hike I had just finished, but whenever I took to the trail. I was overcome with the simplicity of life, energized by the trees, grasslands, and mountains. Going "home" that day was an already accomplished feat. Nature had awakened the kingdom of God within.

THE SPIRITUAL AWAKENING NATURE BRINGS

"Get these glorious works of God into yourself— that's the thing."

—*John Muir*

How does nature effect its spiritual benefits? An analogy about friendship suggests how this takes place. When we are with a true friend, we feel uplifted. Our friend accepts us as we are, responds to us with loving appreciation, and brings out the best in us. We may have forgotten how intelligent or enthusiastic we really are. (People at work or in the daily exchange of living often can only act as a functionary, giving us what we pay for and nothing personal, or acting in the expected manner dictated by roles and culture, status, and position.) A friend, however, inspires us to be our best selves, and mirrors in us qualities the world often neglects.

Years ago I visited a friend who is a housewife with five children. We shared stimulating conversation—I was her window to the world. She eventually returned to college in midlife, obtained her master's degree, and successfully worked as a college reading specialist. In a conversation years later, she remarked that it was our long and stimulating exchanges that gave her the perception of how intelligent she really was, enough to motivate her to return to the university.

Nature acts in a similar manner to help us awaken the spirituality we sometimes leave aside while dealing with the modern world. During a walk around a lake near my summer home in Colorado, I reflected on how nature inspires this spiritual side of us while healing the sometimes stressful lives we bring into the wilderness.

The trail surrounding the lake was clear and firm. While trees ringed the water, accented by cattails, rushes, and tall grasses, the western horizon was open to the soaring mountains of the nearby Indian Peaks Wilderness Area. The firm trail grounded me with its stability; I quickly left my overactive mind and reconnected with my sensual surroundings. The lake mirrored the passing parade of drifting, white, cottonlike summer clouds overhead, inspiring in my soul the same soft calmness. The waters were still, without ripples. I began feeling emptied of all cares, as if in a state of meditation. The Zen masters refer to this as a clear-mindedness.

Nature presented itself as a collage of picturesque paintings and photographs whose composition was perfect with every view—the bent, dark green, leafy branches of the cottonwoods cascading effortlessly into undisturbed water, the snow-crested mountains etching the sky with powerful, upward strokes, the mallards gliding quietly on the lake, and the surrounding hills a backdrop behind the graceful elm and sycamores outlining the waterways. The unfettered scenes nature presented inspired me to feel my own perfection—being on peaceful terms with all I surveyed.

This is one of the insights into how nature spiritualizes us. Each aspect presented to our eye mirrors some aspect of the human condition, but without its prejudicial judgments or fears. Things appear just as they are, simple, uncontrived. The stream next to the lake flowed silently by, reminding me that my life, too, participated in the greater flow of existence in a way that was unfolding as it should be, and that the same creator who directed the waterway next to the lake was also directing me on my journey through life.

The philosophers of the Middle Ages believed that humankind's fulfillment was achieved when each part of our being acted in accordance with its nature. Thus the mind was fulfilled by thinking—reflecting on concepts as if they were literally food for thought. Thomas Aquinas believed that our person was fulfilled by connecting with the awareness of all being surrounding us, the lesser, particular being of this tree, that hill, or a companion drawing us toward the greater infinite being which God is. As I focused on each tree, cloud, bird, scene, etc., as I came to it, I allowed myself to be totally present to what I was observing, trying to grasp the being of God from whence the entire manifestation of nature sprang. My efforts yielded a deeper sense of oneness with all living things, a more complete feeling of peace—the joy of still-mindedness filled with the whole of creation.

Walking through nature, drinking in elixirs of vibrant colors, textures from plants, stone, and soil, and the artistic composition of every scene giving rise to aesthetic pleasures heals us spiritually by dispelling from our consciousness the fears, desires, and thoughts which daily attack our tranquillity. Nature is like visiting an art gallery—the more we pay attention to the beauty of the paintings, the more satisfied is our aesthetic soul. Leaving the world behind means letting go of the conflicts found there.

Nature is especially helpful in grounding us in the present moment. By being present to the scene before us, so much so that we stop thinking of ourselves in terms of anything from our past or future, we release all pain and frustration that comes from leaving the peace of the present moment. We no longer see ourselves as "not having had this or that, not having been this or that, having failed at this or that"—in the present moment found in nature, there is only the peace of what is before us. Being in nature helps us shed every negative identity, role, experience, or frustrated desire. That is why certain moments of childhood and youth are so memorable...we haven't had the chance to create a "life history of painful negative experiences and frustrations."

Along with nature's ability to bring us back into the peace of the "now" is its power to free us from excessive desire. Each time we fixate on wanting something and being aware we don't have it, we create turmoil and stress. When we are hiking through nature, what is there to want? For a time we are freed from desire, because there is nothing to want from or in nature. Nature is all that it is, just as we see and experience it. When we look at a beautiful sunset or sunrise, this truth asserts itself. We enjoy the sunset, are refreshed by it without wanting anything from it. This simple "time out" from being in a culture that thrives in creating wants and desires gives us the needed peace we silently reach for throughout our lives. In nature, for a time, we find it.

NATURE BECOMES OUR TOUCHSTONE

"Get thee up into the high mountains . . . "
—*Isaiah*

Each setting in nature suggests a different spiritual lesson. Mountaineers who ascend the steep, demanding slopes of their attempted peaks know well the power of the mountain. Hiking in the mountainous backcountry in Colorado gives someone a direct lesson in humility. Nature overwhelms us with expansive vistas, soaring peaks, and challenging weather conditions. Yet how much nobler for our human spirit to feel our humility in nature versus standing next to a soaring skyscraper in a busy downtown city. Alpine hiking demands respect for the natural world of mountains and snow. People who have climbed the high peaks feel both awe and reverence for those high places.

Contrast this experience with a trek through barren desert. There the accent is on simplicity, releasing excess attachments, becoming as empty as the surrounding deserts appear to be. All the distractions from civilization are removed. The spiritual challenge, for those who brave the sweeping and seeming emptiness of the desert, is to rebuild the relationship they have with themselves. Freed from what we are not, we are left staring at what we really are, confronting the quantity and quality of love, honor, and respect we have fashioned in our lives toward ourselves and all living things.

A voice from the great expanse asks, "Who do you love?" Many a person has fled the desert to seek the continued distractions of civilization when they were unable to deal with the person they discovered themselves to be. Thus nature at times becomes our touchstone, testing our real character against whatever pretense about ourselves we may have operated from.

If nature is a touchstone for our individual character, it also serves us spiritually in an even more powerful way. Our presence in nature shakes us free from the drone of human mediocrity, the toil of the workplace, and the sameness of any relationships we've allowed to grow stale, and instead instills in us the rejuvenating energy of "love remembered." We again become conscious of the very presence of love in the universe and whether we've allowed love to flow freely from our hearts or remain immobilized by either our fear or our failure to find an object worthy of its bestowal.

While nature serves as a reminder of love present in life and the universe, it also acts as a willing receptacle for some of our deepest feelings. By doing so, nature mirrors its divine heart, reflected in a thousand small and great moments of beauty offered to us across the span of seasons, a heart always open to our longings and need for release—an open and unfettered sharing.

Etty Hillesum, in *An Interrupted Life,* writes that once she "poured out all my tenderness, all the tenderness one cannot express for a man even when one loves him very, very much. I stood on the little bridge and looked across the water; I melted into the landscape and offered all my tenderness up to the sky and the stars and the water....And I felt this was the only way of transforming all the many and deep and tender feelings one carries for another into deeds: to entrust them to nature, to let them stream out under the open spring sky and to realize that there is no other way of letting them go." Even when we find no listening human ear or open human heart, the spiritual love in nature allows for a thousand emotional releases during our sojourn in life.

Go; quietly enter the still forest, walk beside the peaceful lake, a windswept overlook, or a verdant meadow; listen to what the winds of time will bring you out of those still and silent places—voices, feelings, and tears of both human joy and suffering, all cast to the winds, land, and waters, but all done so with the faith that everything surrendered was well received. Nature says "yes" to us—when no one else can or will, and in this we are freed.

As with the realization of God's *Thou* in the universe, nature's love draws us to also glimpse the absolute, but more importantly to offer ourselves to the God that love uncovers, loving without reserve the one object in the universe worthy of that love. St. Augustine's "our hearts are restless till they rest in Thee" finds an honest and true affirmation in the journey we take into nature. Perhaps humanity's deepest and most silent suffering is this quiet agony of his or her love forced to lie dormant because no one worthy appears to accept this great gift. But in the stilled beauty of nature, love draws back the curtain of the universe and reveals the creator whose very love manifests unconditionally around us. We are then invited to taste of our true fulfillment—loving this God with all our heart and mind and strength.

If one's spiritual philosophy also includes the realization that the process of "spiritualization" includes the human spirit reaching beyond itself to become all the good that is within itself to become—then hiking nature's byways indeed proves an ultimate natural balm for the cure of the soul. Our inner balance and wellness are restored by meeting and dialoging with God, being touched by inspirations and healing from love, beauty, and the wisdom-lessons of nature.

The solitude of nature offers us the possibility to set aright any misconceptions about ourselves we may have brought with us. There is great healing in being "left alone," surrounded by an environment that neither judges or falsely praises. This unconditional state of nature, free from personal threat, encourages us to more easily choose to continue our inner work and walk whatever path destiny calls us to. At the same time, we have also been given a deeper appreciation for all life and the land from which it springs. As we heal, we are reminded to work for the good of the planet.

It was this balance achieved between my needing to personally heal and still look outward with service to others that inspired me to form a hiking club for the good of the participants and the subsequent good for the natural world through which we hiked. Mary Oliver writes in "Wild

Geese" (in *Dream Work*) that "You do not have to be good. You do not have to walk on your knees for a hundred miles through the desert repenting. You only have to let the soft animal of your body love what it loves." Becoming one with ourselves includes becoming one with all living things, with the earth. Nature shares its secrets with those who would listen—the spirit discovered within is the same spirit discovered in the temple of nature.

A SENSE OF THE SACRED

"When you walk across the fields with your mind pure and holy, then from all the stones, and all growing things, and all animals, the sparks of their soul come out and cling to you, and they are purified and become a holy fire in you."

—*Hasidic Saying*

The simple truth woven throughout this chapter is that walking into nature brings us into vital contact with a sense of the "sacred"—those elements found in nature that recall to our hearts and minds our spiritual connections, the loving presence of God and our relationship with him, and the love mysteries behind what we see with our physical eyes, along with wisdom and truth. It remains for each of us to act out our spiritual celebration and adoration of the divine presence.

Just picking up a fallen leaf in autumn and admiring its color, the role it played while a part of the tree, its return to the earth, etc., can be an act of worship, our own sacred rite of prayerful celebration; perhaps a vista atop a mountain does the same, or a walk through a stream, a touch and smell of a pine branch, a quiet hush when seeing a deer. Nature, in its sacredness, suggests God, in the elemental mix of earth, wind, water, fire, sky, and all life. The role of hiking is simple—it takes us where we might relate, be healed, touched, inspired, and loved by who and what we truly seek—the God of our deepest yearnings.

MEDITATIONS

Desert Melody

> Coyote played his flute again last night
> His notes drifted across the desert like an eerie moon
> Calling me to dance beneath the stars and offer my
>   bones to the heavens
> White Horse led me to an oasis of calm and I sang
>   my song to the wind
>
> I have never flown on Black Crow's wings
> But I have seen hunger in grown men's eyes
> Women lighting candles in dark sanctuaries
> Children playing in tunnels of human waste
> And I have heard your music and carry it in
>   my dreams
>
> It is the quiet and desperate search for human
>   dignity that shifts the desert sands
> Tall Mesa imprints this history in the blues and
>   violets of its shadowed walls
> The poet, in search of the love that is greater than truth,

Looks to the colors of the setting sun
And is drawn to the mountain

As you have offered me your music, so I must sing
  my song
For there is certain humanity in the offering of one
  soul to another
  —*Alice Brooke McReynolds*

Go out into nature, hike to some near or far place, and meditate, observe, listen to what nature has to say in that place. You might take a notebook, or just remember in your heart what your spirit is told . . . out there. Create your own book of psalms, nature poems, insights, intuitions, and prayers. By taking time out from our busy days, hiking out to some natural setting, we feed our souls with the substance of nature's truths and the love of the creator found in his creation. It doesn't have to be for hours; any time spent in nature is healing. But the key is to come with an open heart and mind, and the ability to see and listen.

We don't have to be in great mountain valleys or see expansive desert vistas from high plateaus. Just a walk into the nearest field or by the closest stream will reward us. Look up—see the outline of the deep green leaves against the blue sky and the flowing white cloud river. It will be enough. Go at dawn's first light, or during the calming shades of twilight; it can be in the dark of a moonless night or in the blaze of the full moon. Nature speaks at all hours, under all conditions, during every season.

The Gift

I can love freely . . . out there,
Among the trees and flowing rivers whose sweet
    waters refresh.
I can love freely . . . out there,
Where the soaring eagle and hawk join with the
    families of geese and duck,
To fill the sky with the flow of life, and catch the
    evening breeze.
I can love freely . . . out there,
Where the green meadows mingle with rainbows of
    wildflowers,
And soaring white waves of cloud dance lively
Or quietly lay in the azure blue sea.
I can love freely . . . out there,
Where desert solitude stills the voices
And releases the memories of the human past.
I can love freely . . . out there,
High up in mountain valleys where peaks surround
    and soar to pierce the sky,
Where no one's fear draws back from my grateful
    embrace,
And Nature's God welcomes my every tear, my
    every sigh . . . and all my love.
I can love freely . . . out there!

—Philip Ferranti

THE DAYHIKING VACATION

Planning How and
Where to Go

"The tendency nowadays to wander in wilderness is delightful to see. Thousands of tired, nerve-shaken, over-civilized people are beginning to find out that going to the mountains is going home; that wildness is a necessity; and that mountain parks and reservations are useful not only as fountains of timber and irrigating rivers, but as fountains of life."

—John Muir, The Wilderness World of John Muir

DAYHIKING: A DAY, A WEEKEND, OR LONGER

Dayhiking for health and wellness is an easy prescription to fill. If you have only a day, take a short one-day mini-vacation on a nearby city or county trail. For weekend dayhiking, go to a not-too-distant state park or wilderness area and set up a base camp from which to do several short hikes. Longer dayhiking vacations can be created using comfortable lodgings as a base from which to hike in national parks or on parts of long-distance trails.

Unique to hiking as an outdoor activity is the diversity and wide extent of land areas available for pursuing this adventurous sport. You can hike wherever there is a trail or wherever the jurisdiction of that land permits off-trail hiking. Mountains, forest, prairie, deserts, seacoast, uplands—trails cross these land features found the world over.

Unlike skiing, dayhiking can be enjoyed year-round. The weather, however, does dictate the kind of hiking you can do and what specialized equipment is needed. Snow hiking with snowshoes or desert hiking in the dead of winter in Death Valley suggests some of the contrasts hiking offers. Trails can be done on a seasonal basis to view the changing colors and flora of nature—brilliant autumn leaves, the hushed silence of fallen snow, the first blush of green along with colorful displays of flowers in spring, and the rich, flowing, full bloom of summer, along with sprays of mountain wildflowers.

Changing weather patterns and different times of day also accent the diversity of hiking. A hike at daybreak is a refreshing new beginning, while late afternoon and early evening hints of a quieter, more reflective moment suggested by the lengthening shadows, the warm rosy-yellow sunlight, and the deeper blue and purple of twilight. Even a full-moon ramble can take you walking through stark desert canyon landscapes of contrasting black and white or enjoying the eerie white brilliance of a snowcapped mountain. Hiking in a storm (John Muir's favorite hiking experiences) can invigorate the spirit, while a soft spring or warm summer rain will calm even the most restless of spirits.

Wherever you hike, even if only a few miles from your home, you can feel as if you're in the midst of a summer vacation. Enjoy the release from stress that hiking offers, the change of scenery, and the challenge of a new experience. Any hike is a kind of mini-vacation, where the cares of the world are laid aside, while the newness of nature replaces the old, stale trappings of civilization. Upon returning to work on Monday, you may be greeted with the tired, letdown look many colleagues wear, while you exude enthusiasm and energy, benefits from having taken to the trail.

PLANNING YOUR OWN HIKING VACATION

For novice hikers and veterans alike, taking a hiking vacation can be one of the most enjoyable and totally healthy experiences one might ever do. A hiking vacation is becoming one of the fastest-growing ways that people are choosing to spend their recreational free time. There are few experiences that offer as many benefits as a hiking vacation. You enjoy a stress-free environment, you exercise, you discover geological, historical, and topographical wonders. The world also makes fewer demands on you while you're hiking, as opposed to dealing with lift lines, hotel crowds, etc., that a ski vacation might encounter.

Hikers discover that being in the wilderness even for just a few hours is truly like taking a vacation. But aside from day or weekend hiking to nearby trails, some of the greatest hiking pleasures come from actually spending one or more weeks on the trail. I'm not talking about backpacking but, rather, planning a trip to one or more hiking areas, car camping or renting a cabin, condo, or hotel room ("gourmet hiking", my favorite way to go), and hiking new trails each day from your base camp.

There are several considerations when planning your own hiking vacation. Depending on the amount of time you have, you can travel to one area and hike there for a week, or if you have several weeks, you might choose at least two different kinds of terrains to hike through, thereby gaining the diversity offered in desert versus mountain hiking or forest versus lowlands.

First, determine how long your vacation will be, and this will help you decide where you want to go. For example, if you have a week, you'll want to go someplace you can get to in a day or less, to ensure at least five days of hiking. If you have two weeks—or more, lucky you!—you can go someplace more remote, say, an Alaskan lake to which you must be flown in, or go on a longer series of hikes such as portions of long-distance trails. Your available time can guide you in choosing from the vast array of hiking choices available. Get information from the nearest U.S. Forest Service center and BLM office (see appendix C, Addresses, at the back of this book). Hiking in these areas can be very rewarding and less crowded than more popular destinations such as national parks.

After you know where you want to hike, pick the right season of the year for the kind of hiking you plan to do. For example, if you have time in early summer, you might consider a hiking vacation to southern Utah, a great place for a spring or autumn adventure; but if your time off is in July or August, southern Utah isn't such a good choice, because summer temperatures can climb into the 100s. On the other hand, a midsummer hike in southern Utah could be done in Zion National Park's Narrows through the Virgin River, where you'll be better assured of being able to do this hike during the medium or low water levels after mid-June. If you have a vacation scheduled for the fall, you'll enjoy certain areas and trails of New England, avoiding black flies and mosquitoes which are swarming from May through July.

Once you've chosen a destination, check with the agency that administers the land where you plan to hike, asking for general information, hiking maps, administrative information (fees, permits required, regulations, etc.). For a list of addresses, see appendix C at the back of this book.

Find out more about the area near the trails you'll be hiking. Get the phone number of the local Chamber of Commerce or the nearest large town, and ask for lodging and sightseeing information. Is there a good grocery store in town to replenish your hiking supplies? Do you want to know about restaurants, art galleries, etc.? Ask for hiking and outdoor recreational materials; you may discover other places you would want to hike through, even if away from your original destination.

Plan well ahead, and make any reservations for camping or lodging or hiking permits as soon as you possibly can. Lodgings in or near national parks, for instance, are sometimes filled six months to a year in advance!

Get a book on the area you plan to visit and read about your destination beforehand; a hiking and outdoor recreational guide will do well. You might discover something worth exploring, or at least get an appreciation about the places you will be traveling to. Besides your local bookstore or library, you can get books from the Adventurous Traveler Bookstore (800-282-3963), a mail-order company carrying thousands of outdoor titles with salespeople who are experienced hikers. Recreational Equipment Inc. (REI) is also a great source for both books and tips about the equipment you might be needing.

Make an equipment, clothing, and food list in advance. For the basics on dayhiking needs, consult a good how-to guide such as those mentioned in "Dayhiking: How to Get Started," in chapter 1, Hiking: The Ultimate Natural Prescription for Health and Wellness. Make sure that you bring only what is actually needed. Favor "less" rather than "more" and go light; as you'll discover once you're in or near wilderness, your needs are far less than you might have thought.

What a Hiking Vacation Looks Like:
Zion National Park

Zion National Park in southwestern Utah is 229 square miles of sculptured canyons and plateaus. Native Indians felt that this collection of scenic canyons accented by pine, cottonwood, and wildflowers was a very spiritual place, an opinion so strongly shared by the first Mormons who saw the canyons that they named them Zion, after the biblical reference to heaven and paradise. Everyone has their own special interests, and you can easily adjust the following possible scenario for your own dayhiking vacation.

You've chosen Zion National Park because you want to explore the colorful southwest canyon country of Utah. Good choice! This is an incredibly beautiful area you've often heard about and you are excited about seeing it for yourself. After researching the climate conditions of the area, you decide the best time to go is in the fall, so you arrange your vacation time accordingly. You will be in Zion from September 15 to 25, and you'll have ten days of actual vacation time once at Zion. To save money, you are going to camp in the national park for three days, then rent a nice hotel room in Springdale, the town adjacent to Zion. You make your camping and hotel reservations well in advance.

When you arrive at Zion National Park, you first inquire at the visitors center for the latest information on the hiking trails and weather conditions. You discover that the park has a shuttle service to trailheads located at various points throughout the park. This helps you decide your itinerary for the three days that you are camping in the park. You go set up a base camp at your reserved campsite.

For your first hike, you take a park service shuttle to the park's east entrance to do the scenic 10-mile East Rim Trail. The hike fills you with wonder and excitement at discovering the fantastic sandstone formations and canyons of Zion. The hike brings you back to Zion Canyon, where you take another park service shuttle back to your campsite.

The next day you explore the easy trails in Zion Canyon itself. These hikes can be reached from your campsite or by driving just 2 or 3 miles, so you have a refreshingly vehicle-minimal day!

On the third day, you visit the local art galleries in Springdale and drive to nearby St. George to explore the town. You discover that on the mountains west of St. George is a well-developed network of hiking trails. You begin to think of other hiking you might want to do during this vacation.

On the fourth day you break camp and return to Springdale, where you check into your comfortable hotel, with pool and Jacuzzi, for your next seven days' lodging. After settling in to your new base "camp," you return to the national park and hike the famous Narrows of the Virgin River, a round trip of 6 miles through a river surrounded by spectacular and colorful canyon walls. At the time of year you are visiting, this river only comes up to your knees at the very deepest places.

On day 5 you drive 80-plus miles to Bryce Canyon National Park and spend the day hiking the 8-mile Fairyland Trail through fantastic hoodoos (exotic rock formations). You return to Springdale ready for a soak in the Jacuzzi and a good night's sleep.

On day 6 you drive to the Kaibab Plateau in northern Arizona, to the North Rim of the Grand Canyon, almost 140 miles away, and discover the conditions there less crowded than at the South Rim. You stop at the visitors center and pick up some great hiking books about the Kaibab Plateau and the more than 250 miles of hiking trails that cross it. Then you do an easy-to-moderate hike along the North Rim, the Widforss Trail, which offers good views of the canyon. You could also have chosen from the more than 50 miles of the Kaibab Plateau Trail, which crosses the plateau through some of its scenic forest landscape. You return to Springdale for the night.

On day 7 you take a break from hiking and revisit St. George, take an historical tour, shop, and spend the day sightseeing. You enjoy dinner in St. George before returning to your hotel in Springdale.

On day 8 you drive 50 to 75 miles to take a hike in the nearby Dixie National Forest, which breaks up your exposure to sandstone canyons. Here, the trails take you through forests of ponderosa, juniper, and pine, a cooler alternative to canyon hiking. Your hotel in Springdale is a welcome sight after a long day of forest wandering.

On day 9 you rest again, do final shopping and sightseeing in Springdale, and prepare for the best hike of all, the 14-mile Lava Point Trail.

On day 10 you take another shuttle for the long but magnificent Lava Point hike. This spectacular 14-mile trail takes you through the heart of Zion National Park for a scenic look at the great canyons in Zion's backcountry. Lava Point is, at almost 8,000 feet, the highest elevation in Zion National Park. The trailhead is surrounded by bright and dark shades of green foliaged trees, mostly aspen and pine. (Sadly, a fire in July 1996 burned much of the foliage along the first seven miles of this trail.)

The first 6 miles follow along the very top of the long, narrow Horse Pasture Plateau, in places no wider than 100 yards. The plateau drops off into flanks of flowing pine and shrub that eventually meet distant mountains, other nearby plateaus, and a collection of some of the most stunning canyons found anywhere in nature. The colors waken your senses, as deep purple, gray, and brown lava are accented by the azure sky and the covering green sheet of pine and other foliage. The trail opens to all horizons, permitting you to look out for miles into the surrounding Utah deserts, mountains and canyons.

Within a few miles you reach a lookout point that opens to the first great side canyon that comes into the plateau, the left fork of North Creek. The creek has scoured out a magnificent canyon, the length of which you can look down from your vantage point along Lava Point Trail, while picking out rock formations, trees along the creekbed, and the impressive Pine Mountains that loom above the town of St. George to the southwest.

After almost 4 miles the trail drops down into a small depression known as Potato Hollow. The hollow is an island of green amidst the surrounding colorful but sparsely vegetated canyons. The next section of trail follows the edge of the plateau and offers a series of canyon vistas from all the side canyons that flow down from or into the plateau. Few trails have such a spectacular backdrop.

The trail continues until you begin descending almost 3,000 feet into the lower canyons of Zion's backcountry. Once off the plateau, you make your way quickly along the creek and eventually onto a long section of trail etched into the red-hued sandstone plateau that borders above Zion Canyon. The hike ends as you wind your way down the final section of plateau and mountain trail. The trail here gives you a view of the entire Zion valley as it opens up to the mouth of the canyon. Looking down, you can see the Virgin River washing through the canyon floor, the banks rich with generous stands of cottonwoods and grasses, a fitting end to this incredible journey. Zion—truly nature's hint of heavenly places.

The next day you head back to "civilization," having hiked more than 60 miles over a ten-day period, feeling energized, wanting to return at your next opportunity, and glad you chose to vacation this way. Depending on your lodgings and meals, the total cost per person is about $450.

What Another Hiking Vacation Looks Like:
The Southwest's Four Corners Area
Several friends shared with me their experiences of three weeks hitting the trails. "We began in Zion National Park. What a discovery that was! I felt especially good about being able to hike through the canyons and not just on top of them. The colors, rock formations, and views were breathtaking, while the climate was mild enough; we were hiking at elevations of between 8,000 and 4,000 feet, which we found to be quite comfortable. And it was so nice to swim in the afternoons after 10- to 12-mile hikes.

"We went on to Moab, Utah, and visited both Canyonlands and Arches National Parks. Canyonlands gave us some of the most fantastic vistas we've ever seen— you could look for miles across southeastern Utah from the rim trails that follow the edges of its many plateaus.

"From there we traveled into Colorado for a taste of the high country, and stayed in Ouray, a beautiful mountain town surrounded by soaring mountains. The whole area was referred to as the Switzerland of America. We did some scenic climbs on trails that took us over 13,000 feet in elevation. The mountain wildflowers were more beautiful than I've seen anywhere. It was quite a change from the canyons and deserts of Utah, but that is what we liked, the contrast and different temperatures, wildlife and lush green forests.

"A hike through Yankee Boy Basin was the highlight of our mountain hiking. Not only was the land scenic with mountains, but sprinkled alongside the trail were many remains of old mines that took us back to historical flavors of the late 1800s.

"After I got home, I felt like I had been away for months! It was a whole new world, a different kind of experience. All winter I read up on geology and the Colorado Plateau, and planned another adventure for next summer. Being in that kind of landscape really opened me up to just how much of this country I've yet to see. My friends agreed that hiking was a great way to discover America."

OTHER POSSIBILITIES

The above hiking vacation scenarios are just two of many possibilities open to those who choose dayhiking as a recreational vacation. Costs are much lower than other traditional kinds of vacations. You also stand a good chance of improving your health and well-being by hiking for one, two, or more weeks. Because your "territory" is so extensive, you can combine several different trips into one.

Some possibilities, limited only by your interest and enthusiasm, might include hiking in several national parks; doing some river rafting and canoeing as a part of your hiking experience; going on archaeological or historical-based hiking trips; hiking sections of a major national trail, without necessarily backpacking; hiking the premier state parks in the state where you choose to vacation; visiting the backcountry trails in out-of-the-way scenic areas; doing a llama trek, where your gear is packed in by llama; and setting up a base camp from where you can hike a variety of nearby trails. The next several sections describe some of these other kinds of hiking vacations.

Guided Hiking

If planning your own hiking vacation sounds like too much work, you can choose to go on a hiking vacation where someone else has planned your itinerary, you stay each night in a cozy, comfortable lodge, hotel, or bed-and-breakfast, and the bulk of your gear is carried by some conveyance other than yourself. These kinds of hiking vacations are rapidly increasing in popularity, with over 100 companies offering a variety of trips to locations in and out of the United States. The hikes (or walks, as they are often called) are designed for the endurance level of the participants. They can range from short 5-mile rambles to more strenuous 20-mile-plus adventures.

If you go on any guided trip, ask to be put in contact with people who have taken the same trip and inquire about their impressions, advice, and what they found most helpful in enjoying their hiking vacation. What can a vacationer expect on these guided hiking trips? A representative company for these kinds of tours is New England Hiking Holidays (800-869-0949). This outfitter has an impressive list of destinations; they comfort the potential hiker with the assertion that "We always have two guides per trip to accommodate both slower and faster walkers and to appeal to the casual but enthusiastic walker as well as the experienced hiker. Our groups are small and personal (around sixteen people per trip) and our experienced guides are always eager to share their love and knowledge of the natural world. What an array of fine inns we have for you. Whether it's an exquisitely restored, fifteenth-century highwayman's inn or a luxurious, more modern mountaintop chalet, we are sure you'll enjoy the comforts and hospitality of your accommodations. Fine food and great beds really top off a day of hiking." For a listing of other companies that offer guided dayhiking, see Appendix C, Addresses.

Heli-Hiking

A more adventurous approach to the dayhiking vacation is heli-hiking, in which you are dropped off in remote wilderness areas by helicopter, where you hike until the return rendezvous with the helicopter, which returns you to a comfortable lodge. One such company in this field is Canadian Mountain Holidays Heli-Hiking (800-661-0252). They specialize in wilderness destinations in and near the Canadian Rocky Mountains. Vacationers choose to stay and hike from one lodge, or from lodge to lodge, and can opt for photography workshops or combination hiking, biking, and canoeing. The uniqueness of this kind of trip is being "delivered to wilderness that would otherwise be almost impossible to access. With your guide you explore a spectacular landscape of high alpine ridges, abundant wildflowers, glaciers, and turquoise mountain lakes."

Llama Trekking

For a real change of pace, try llama trekking. On these vacations, llamas pack your gear for you, walking alongside while you hike the wilderness, with guides providing all the cooking and camp setup. This is more of a true wilderness experience, minus the heavy load of a backpack. You might even become friends with your llama! Contact the Chamber of Commerce nearest to the area you want to hike in for information about local llama trekking outfitters. You can also contact the International Llama Association (see Appendix C, Addresses).

Canoeing and Hiking

Combining the pleasures of several outdoor pursuits is what a canoeing and hiking vacation is all about. Clearwater Canoe Outfitters (800-527-0554), representative of this kind of vacation package, specializes in outfitting the Boundary Waters Canoe Area of Minnesota and Ontario's Quetico Park. Vacationers can choose to camp or enjoy the amenities of a lodge, but either way, all equipment and food is provided, along with any required instruction. Once on your way, you can base-camp while hiking the nearby trails. For hiking enthusiasts who love the quiet peace of a mountain lake or gentle rivers, this vacation combination has much to offer. For other outfitters, contact America Outdoors (see Appendix C, Addresses, at the back of this book).

Bicycling and Hiking
Combining the pleasures of several outdoor pursuits is also what a bicycling and hiking vacation is all about. Backroads (800-245-3874), representative of this kind of vacation package, guides tours all over the country, of varying duration and difficulty. Vacationers can choose to camp or enjoy the amenities of a lodge. While cycling you can cover more ground and get from one hiking destination to another; and dayhiking offers a welcome respite from the bicycle seat!

CREATE YOUR OWN HIKING LIFESTYLE

Hiking offers quick pick-you-up benefits that often encourage a person to change their lifestyle to include at least one hike a week. Hiking vacations are anticipated as rejuvenating and adventurous holidays, but hiking on a weekly basis provides a consistent lifestyle return of positive experiences.

Time management experts often conclude that if someone wants to do something badly enough, they have to organize their time and prioritize their responsibilities toward achieving the desired activity. Hiking is no different. But, unlike many outdoor activities or sports, hiking gives the participant plenty of leeway for scheduling a hike.

During months of extended daylight, many people can arrive home in time for a late afternoon or early evening hike. Pick a destination close enough to home for a quick drive, and you can be on the trail within minutes of leaving home. Plan to take a picnic dinner or have something cooked ahead, and you have the makings of a midweek holiday anytime you like. In my club, there are midafternoon hikes from 2:00 to 8:00 p.m. Each afternoon we drive from near-100-degree temperatures in the desert town where we live to a cool 70 degrees in the nearby mountains for hikes at between 6,000 and 9,000 feet. With a group dinner afterward in a mountain resort town, these afternoon jaunts become the high point for many during the work week.

Many people schedule hikes around a flexible work schedule, including teachers who arrive home in late afternoon; nurses who work shifts that allow for an entire morning or afternoon off; people with four-day work weeks that allow at least one of three "weekend" days for hiking; businesspeople who schedule meetings and work to free them for a late afternoon hike; homemakers who set aside a three- or four-hour (or more) block of time once a week for hikes with family, friends, or a hiking group; and couples who arrange a time together each or every other week to hike. Many arrange to finish early what they have to do at work, or take advantage of comp time owed them.

For me, all I have to do is remember how good I feel after every hike, and I become highly motivated to arrange my time for hiking every week. It's a matter of priorities. Nor is hiking restricted to the regular workday. There are several days each month that allow for full-moon hikes during late evening hours. The hiking club I belong to schedules these full-moon rambles monthly, with sometimes twenty-five to thirty-five people participating—many coming after a full day's work, but always finishing the hike feeling far better than when they started. It's also possible to hike at first daylight, especially if you have to report to work after 10:00 a.m. These sunrise hikes are a great way to start the day, energize your work, and generally set yourself up for having a positive and wonderful day.

The hiking lifestyle centers around one simple guiding principle: get outdoors on some kind of trail at least once a week. It can be an open space or riverwalk trail, a long walk through the local park, a drive out to the nearest quiet country road to hike along the roadway where traffic is light, a quick trip to the nearest foothill, mountain, or oceanfront trail. Sometimes it's just a simple walk through the tall prairie grasses, or along a desert canyon wash. But make that commitment to be out-of-doors, in nature, hiking whatever path presents itself, and the benefits will flow to you with every step you take.

DISCOVERING LOCAL TRAILS

Most city dwellers, along with small-town residents, can reach nature within a reasonable drive from their home. Even just driving out into the nearby countryside and walking down a country road will provide many of the benefits that come from hiking. But there are usually hiking trails, built through lands under the stewardship of a variety of government agencies. City and county parks and recreation districts sometimes provide trail systems virtually in one's own backyard. Urban trail systems include open space lands usually set aside by city or county governments as well as trails built alongside rivers that pass through cities, sometimes referred to as river walkways.

The Bay Area Ridge Trail (described below), while representing one of the better marriages of trail and city, also underscores the availability of trail systems near many American metropolitan areas. Boston has its Berkshires, White, and Green Mountains, New York its Catskills and Adirondacks, Washington, DC, its Appalachian Trail and Shenandoah Valley, Denver its Rocky Mountains, Chicago its Ice Age Trail, etc. These trail systems and wilderness areas are close enough to their respective urban centers to allow plentiful hiking.

Ask your local parks department or at any good outdoor equipment or sporting goods store about local trail information, ask at bookstores, or contact the nearest hiking club. Chapters of the Sierra Club are one of the best resources for finding where the trails are located. In other parts of the country, especially in the West, the U.S. Forest Service maintains offices in urban areas and can provide generous amounts of information and maps for those hiking areas near and far from urban centers. See Appendix C, Addresses, at the back of this book.

An Urban Sampler:
The Bay Area Ridge Trail, California
The following is a sample of just how close urban dwellers are to great hiking, sometimes minutes away. Many other American cities tell a similar story, but you will have to do some investigation to discover these hiking treasures.

People vacationing in San Francisco are drawn to its culture, refinement, ethnic diversity, and great restaurants. Yet, surrounding San Francisco and the adjacent cities of

Oakland, San Jose, and Berkeley is a magnificent, scenic marriage of mountains, ocean, and bay, joined together by mountains of the Coastal Range and the rolling foothills and valleys that spread down from their flanks.

An impressive trail system known as the Bay Area Ridge Trail runs atop the surrounding ring of ridgeline and through nearby open spaces. The Bay Area Ridge Trail, when completed, will allow the entire Bay Area to be hiked and enjoyed to the fullest, from Sonoma, Napa Valley, and Santa Rosa, down through Marin County, Stinson Beach, Mount Tamalpais, and Muir Woods, through San Francisco and over the ridge of mountains running down the Peninsula through stunning redwood forests and over to the East Bay and back up to Napa Valley. Almost 200 miles have been completed of this 400-mile multi-use trail, allowing access to anyone within 30 miles from the trail. Bay Area residents and visitors who hike this trail are treated to a mild year-round climate and a wide range of oak-accented grasslands, redwood forests, wooded creeks tinted with bright green moss and the famous California spring wildflowers.

It is this kind of trail network, close to a large urban area of 6 million people, that encourages people to enjoy the true flavors of a weekend hiking vacation. Spectacular hiking abounds just minutes from any Bay Area resident's front door. From the vineyards of Napa-Sonoma to the redwood forests along the mountains south of San Francisco, hiking opportunities allow for a quick entry into nature's bounty.

I spent one Memorial Day weekend hiking the Russian Ridge portion of the Bay Area Ridge Trail, a moderate 6-mile hike. I was overwhelmed and impressed by the beauty, rich diversity of scenery, and incredible mix of ocean views, grasslands, and forests scented with redwood, pine, flowers, and sea breezes.

STATE PARKS

Besides local and county park and trail information, each state has developed state parks where usually you can find a variety of hiking trails. For example, Colorado has forty state parks with over 600 miles of hiking trails. These trails are in parks that are accessible for most people within a two-hour drive from their home. Many hiking treasures are hidden within state park systems and are worth discovering. Call any state's capitol for state park information. For a sampling of state parks, see the "Selected State Parks" section of Appendix C, Addresses, at the back of this book.

A State Park Sampler: The Frazer Trail,
Golden Gate Canyon State Park, Colorado
The Frazer Meadow Trail is a rewarding adventure, especially during late spring or early fall. Golden Gate Canyon State Park is only 25 miles from Denver, and the drive through the Front Range mountains quickly introduces you to Colorado's high country. A mix of horse ranches and farms accent the journey into the park, with a spectacular view of the Continental Divide just before you reach the park entrance.

The 9-mile (round-trip) Frazer Trail is located less than 1 mile north of the visitors center. You begin by following a creek up a narrow canyon lined with aspen and pine. As the trail climbs, a glance back to the east reveals the soaring mountains that form the eastern park boundary. Further along the trail, as it follows the ridgeline up to higher elevations, there are overlooks.

Columbines, the Colorado state flower, and aspen border the trail. Eventually, after just over 1 mile of hiking, you emerge on a plateau filled with an aspen forest. During a fall hike, this forest becomes a sea of yellow. Another 0.5 mile of hiking brings you into Frazer Meadows.

If you are fortunate enough to take this hike during June, you will be treated to hundreds of purple iris scattered through the rich green grasses of one of the largest meadows in any of Colorado's state parks. The remains of Frazer's cabin home accent the trail and meadow, with old farm equipment from 100 years ago placed nearby by Colorado State Parks to authenticate the setting. The views from the meadow are expansive, highlighting the surrounding peaks and brilliant white clouds usually billowing up over the mountains during most summer days.

The trail continues higher up, passing through several pine forests before finally surprising you with a spectacular vista at the trail's end, appropriately named Panorama Point. From here, hikers can see the Rocky Mountains and the Continental Divide, from Rocky Mountain National Park to the north all the way to the row of 14,000-foot peaks that border Interstate 70 to the south. The hike is comfortable, and a great beginning to any hiking vacation in Colorado.

NATIONAL PARKS AND LANDS

Several federal agencies oversee thousands of miles of most wilderness-based hiking trails. The National Park Service is the most famous of the national recreational agencies, and oversees 14,000 miles of hiking trails throughout the United States. Contact National Park Service headquarters in Washington, DC (see appendix C, Addresses) and ask for hiking information and the map to the entire National Park System. You may also contact the National Park Service regional office (regional offices are also listed in appendix C, Addresses), and you can contact the national park where you intend to visit for maps and park and hiking information. For a sample of what a dayhiking vacation to a national park might look like, see "A National Lands Sampler: "Indian Peaks Wilderness Area" later in this chapter.

The U.S. Forest Service manages the country's largest trail network, with over 105,000 miles of hiking trail. This agency has built a massive trail system throughout the national forests that they govern; many of their trails link up with Bureau of Land Management or state park trail systems adjacent to national forest service land. To contact the Forest Service for information, see appendix C, Addresses, at the back of this book.

The Bureau of Land Management (BLM) has almost 4,000 miles of trails (and much more if you consider the possibility of hiking off trail in wilderness areas) scattered through 240 million acres of land located mostly in the western United States. The BLM publishes excellent maps and other information, including a map called "Recreation Guide to BLM Public Lands" and "National Recreation Guide" that highlights the location of both trail systems and recreational opportunities nationwide. For information, see appendix C, Addresses, for the national office and a listing of all BLM state offices.

Hiking trails can also be found in national monuments, nature preserves, even along old sections of unused railroad beds which are being converted to hiking trails.

A National Lands Sampler: The Devil's Thumb Trail, Indian Peaks Wilderness Area, Colorado

The Indian Peaks Wilderness Area, located south of Rocky Mountain National Park and west of Boulder, Colorado, offers the hiker several hundred miles of trail to enjoy, from the lower foothill elevations of 7,000 to 9,000 feet, to the top of the Continental Divide and along its many 12,000- to 13,000-foot peaks. One of my favorite trails is the Devil's Thumb Trail, named after a rock outcropping that resembles somebody's thumb.

This hike is typical for Colorado. You leave the lowlands, access a trailhead at a much higher elevation, and then begin a great hike through subalpine forests and eventually to the peak line of some awe-inspiring mountain range, with a view that makes you wonder why you ever have to leave.

The Devil's Thumb Trail, a 15-mile round-trip hike, begins at the Hessie Trailhead, outside the quaint mountain town of Eldora. The trail climbs along a section of gravel road that offers spectacular views of the Eldora Ski Area to the south, as well as expansive mountain valleys filled with several old cabins and surrounding forests of aspen and Douglas fir that spread out in all directions, while leaving some magnificent rock outcroppings exposed. Soon you arrive at the juncture of South Fork Creek. Here a roaring river cascades down a series of falls and seems to say "welcome to the high country."

The Devil's Thumb Trail veers up and to the right of the river. After a short, hard climb through a fir and pine forest, the trail begins to level out and empties into an expansive meadow. The surrounding views are inspiring. Directly in front and still miles away is a circular bowl of snowcapped mountains. Breathtaking in their beauty and grandeur, they form a kind of magnet that draws you toward what you know is the inevitable reward of summiting the Continental Divide. The valley through which the trail follows is wide enough to give you the feeling of openness and freedom. The meadow overflows with red and orange Indian paintbrush, blue and purple lupine, larkspur, and an assortment of yellow wildflowers that brilliantly contrast with the deep green grass of early summer.

Especially appealing are the stately forests of Douglas fir, spruce, and pine. The trees close at hand are separated enough so that their full regal stature can be appreciated, while the main forest begins several hundred yards away and sweeps up all the surrounding mountainsides. This section of trail is energizing in its majestic beauty and provides an authentic Colorado signature to the hike.

Proceeding 1 mile further brings you to a roaring waterfall flowing down the mountainside to the left. The trail now becomes a section of what was probably once a mining road. Old logs still form the trailbed, while a torrent of water, especially in late spring and early summer, gushes over and down the trail. You must choose your footing carefully here or, if wet boots are of no concern, plod up the trail for more than 0.25 mile before it levels out, free from any moving water.

The hike gradually draws you into a narrowing mountain valley. After enjoying the trek through more forest, you come to Jasper Lake, where you can sit and take in the scenic alpine lake setting. Colorado is a land filled with trails leading to high alpine lakes. The geology and geography dictate that as snow melts it will gather in the first depressions large enough to hold it—hence the many lakes in the high country. These lakes then drain by streams, creeks, or small rivers down to lower valleys and lakes before these waterways drop down into either the High Plains or the larger mountain-born rivers of the Colorado Plateau.

In the deep blue skies of Colorado's high country, the pure white clouds begin massing in early afternoon from moisture that flows north from the Gulf of Mexico. These are cottonball-types, well defined, great free-flowing gobs of white cumulus that form in the skies overhead, and dominate the mountain ridges along the horizon. Colorado mountains form a perfect backdrop for highlighting the beauty and grace of these soaring white clouds. The Rockies are often a mix of gray, cream, red, rust, brown, and purple rock brought to sharp relief by the mantle of deep green Douglas fir and spruce that cover the higher slopes. The pure white of the massive cloud formations contrast these sharper colors, and are in turn set off by the Colorado azure sky.

This parade of white clouds that suddenly appears over the mountain ridges can signal a cooler flow of air approaching, and after a long, sometimes hot hike up the mountain, this is welcome relief. You would have to live in an area of the country that is usually void of these kinds of clouds to fully appreciate the effects they have on the human spirit. In my home desert, clear skies are the rule, and a cumulus formation is indeed a rarity. In other parts of the country great sheets of clouds often cover the entire sky, leaving few occasions for the individual massive cumulus parades to ever get organized. But in Colorado's high country, you can always count on summer buildups of the big white puffballs.

The Devil's Thumb Trail offers plenty of opportunities to cloud-watch. After leaving Jasper Lake and climbing through the last forest to Devil's Thumb Lake, you are greeted by an expansive opening of mountains and peaks formed in a bowl shape, and marking the boundary for the Continental Divide. The trail brings you past the lake and into subalpine terrain, where only small trees and ground cover exist. A hard climb up switchbacks takes you out of the bowl and onto the High Lonesome Trail, which for miles follows the peak line of the Divide.

From the top, at almost 12,000 feet, you can look for miles across Colorado's high-country mountains. Sometimes you stand virtually in the clouds; other times you are gazing across a cloudless sky at countless snowcapped peaks stretching all the way to what seems to be the Utah border.

LONG-DISTANCE NATIONAL TRAILS

America is covered by some of the most scenic national trails found anywhere in the world. A great dayhiking vacation would be to travel a section of one or more of these trails, camping or staying in lodges so that you could dayhike opposite directions along the trail. By contacting the American Hiking Society (see appendix C, Addresses), you can get information on the organizations that support these national trails and on the trails themselves.

Some of these long and scenic national trails include the Appalachian Trail on the eastern seaboard; the Pacific Crest Trail linking Canada to Mexico via California's Sierra Nevadas and Oregon and Washington's Cascade Range; the Continental Divide Trail following the Divide throughout the Rocky Mountains; the Lewis and Clark Trail following the explorers' route from St. Louis, Missouri to Oregon; the Ice Age Trail linking almost 1,000 miles of Wisconsin scenic trail; the Natchez Trail from Nashville, Tennesee, to Natchez, Mississippi; the Santa Fe Trail from Missouri to New Mexico; the North Country Trail from New York to North Dakota; and the American Discovery Trail California to Delaware.

A Long-Distance Trail Sampler:
The American Discovery Trail
The proposed 6,000 miles of the American Discovery Trail will cross America from Point Reyes and San Francisco in California to Cape Henlopen in Delaware. The trail's 2,000 completed miles pass through or near Reno, Nevada; Moab, Utah; Grand Junction and Denver, Colorado. It then splits into two routes, one going through Omaha, Nebraska; Davenport, Iowa; and near Chicago, Illinois, to Cincinnati, Ohio. The other route goes through Kansas City, Kansas; St. Louis, Missouri; and Evansville, Illinois, before reconnecting in Cincinnati and proceeding to Washington, DC, and the Atlantic Coast.

BUILDING THE FUTURE

The Care and Enjoyment
of the Earth

*"What do you suppose will satisfy the soul, except
to walk free and own no superior?"*

—Walt Whitman

The demographics of America are changing, and lifestyles are following that change. America is aging, while at the same time senior citizens are living much healthier lives. Gone is the "little ol' lady in the rocking chair" image that once characterized the older American. The baby boomers, who represent a population bulge of 76 million, have grown up with more interest in sports and outdoor pursuits than any other generation. They popularized golf, tennis, running, backpacking, etc. Their influence has been felt in other generations as well, with mountain biking, rock climbing, and other sports now on the rise in the generation following the boomers. The effects of these trends in the future are that outdoor recreation will increase in importance to overshadow all other types of sports or health-promoting activities.

Other trends affecting how we recreate are also being identified. Those individuals who engaged in the more demanding sports such as jogging will probably be looking for a less-impact-on-your-joints kind of activity. Tennis players and eventually mountain bikers as they age will most likely follow suit. Any injury to elbows will hinder golfers and some of them will make the switch as well. But into what?

Into dayhiking—the one outdoor activity that is on the rise faster than all others, with already over 42 million Americans calling themselves hikers and almost 150 million Americans indicating that they walk for exercise some part of every week. Between 1982 and 1995, hiking was the fastest-growing outdoor activity, with a growth rate of almost 100 percent for people over the age of sixteen. As our population ages, individuals will turn to activities that offer less chance of injury, can be done under a wide variety of conditions, and yet still provide a full physical exercise workout. Dayhiking is that activity.

The National Trails Agenda Project was begun in 1988 as a cooperative venture between the National Park Service and American Trails (an organization under the auspices of the American Hiking Society) to look at trail issues and develop recommendations to satisfy America's current and future trail needs. The project asks, "What would it take for all Americans to be able to go out their front doors and within fifteen minutes be on trails that wind through their cities, towns, or villages and bring them back without retracing steps? Along the way they could pass shops and restaurants, go to work, school, or a park, visit a historic site or the zoo, and experience the great outdoors without a car or bus. If they were to follow the right path, the trail would take them into the countryside or possibly link up with another trail that would lead them into the deepest wilderness or to the highest mountain or across the widest prairie. They would travel across America on trails that connect one community to another and stretch from coast to coast, and from border to border. To form a national system, trails must be viewed as part of the nation's physical infrastructure and included along with highways, utility and sewer lines, airports, and other public facilities as part of the general conduct of everyday governance; trails must be seen in the larger context of the corridors and environments through which they pass; corridor protection must be the primary goal; and the highest priority in developing such a system must be in close-to-home areas, particularly where resources are closest to population centers. The creation of a true national system of trails begins with all Americans in their own backyards—in neighborhoods and communities, in churches, schools, and social organizations, in cities and towns, in every country and state. All Americans are called upon to act. . . . "

This national trails network is now being created, but it is still in its infancy. We already have a growing number of long-distance trails that will take hikers through the finest outdoor wilderness in America. But much more is needed.

Americans living in the urban sprawl that accounts for 75 percent of the population need to exit the concrete jungle and get into the immediate and nearby green open spaces, fields, parks, etc., that will provide them a welcome relief from the congested stress of city life. These trails will be designed for use by all Americans, including senior citizens, children, families, teens, groups, and the physically challenged, and designed for all uses, such as walking, hiking, horseback riding, cross-country skiing, skateboarding, bicycling, backpacking, roller blading, etc. Diversity of trail types will accent the entire system. From a land-scaped, urban bikepath where children safely walk or bicycle to school, or a former railroad line through the woods where classes and youth groups can go for exercise and ecology lessons, to a riverwalk where citizens can meet and stroll to shops, theaters, and restaurants, or a community greenway where families and individuals can walk or exercise at fitness stations, or greenbelts that whisk you away from the cities and towns into the surrounding countryside, linking you up with trail networks that travel to all corners of your state's forests, national trails, BLM recreational areas, state parks, regional trail systems or conservation and nature preserves. Nature, and traveling through its rejuvenating byways, will then occupy the rightful place in our national culture, psyches, and lifestyles, helping us balance and improve our health, mental fitness, civility toward each other, physical conditioning, and spirituality.

The need for trails and their increased use would be greatly enhanced if the national attitude toward land and its use would "evolve" toward what Sweden now enjoys. According to the Swedish Embassy, the "Swedes are a nation of nature-lovers. One illustration of this is the 'right of common access' which allows everyone to roam more or less as they please through the countryside. Sweden is one of the few countries in the world with this right of common access. This is not legally enacted but rather an unwritten 'inviolable right.' The only 'private' areas are those in the immediate vicinity of houses and holiday residences, and where crops are grown. Thus the general public may go wherever it wants as long as it does not encroach on people's privacy and does not damage or disrupt nature."

This right of common access does not always apply to nature reserves, other protected zones, or certain reserves and bird sanctuaries completely closed to visitors during the sensitive breeding season. However, this "everyman's right," as it is called, "involves not only freedoms but also duties and responsibilities. Littering is forbidden, as is tree-felling and breaking branches, twigs, or bark from living trees. Open fires may not be lit in dry terrain or on bare rock. Tents may be pitched where they will not disturb local dwellers or be harmful to nature. Off-road driving is prohibited when there is no snow on the ground. Fishing is allowed along the coast and in the country's five largest lakes; elsewhere permits are required. You are entitled to pick wild berries, flowers, and mushrooms, and to take fallen branches from the ground, but certain rare flowers may not be picked. Take all litter with you and tidy up after yourself when leaving any area of nature."

This common-sense approach of Sweden contrasts sharply with the antagonism too often seen between the land owners and recreational users of America. It's time to adopt a national policy of civility, mutual respect, freedom, responsibility, and common rights of access and use.

INVOLVEMENT IS THE KEY

People protect and enhance what they enjoy and find valuable. Our challenge is not only to build trails and conserve wilderness and open spaces, but to encourage people to actively visit and hike in these resources. I believe that a local, state, and national emphasis on "hiking" and outdoor "use" would go a long way toward insuring the proper conservancy and use of our natural heritage. When political issues surface, the many users of the trails and outdoors would rise as one voice in protecting nature's bounty.

Public and Private Education
One yet-to-be-heard-from resource in this effort is public and private education. State Departments of Education might consider recommendations that would encourage this exposure to the outdoors via outdoor recreation.

First, they could create a curriculum from elementary through high school that includes nature studies and related topics. Include ecology, natural history, plant and animal life, a reemphasis on geography, field trips to wilderness areas, and hiking as a valid physical education sport. Especially in high school, make accommodations for hiking as a part of the curriculum, either as an elective or related course of studies leading to a career in outdoor education, outdoor recreation, land management, etc.

Second, they should give teachers the support and ability to sponsor hikes or weekend trips with their students to learn hiking, camping, backpacking, canoeing, rock climbing, skiing, etc. These are activities that will serve them for a lifetime, offer them intense physical exercise, social interaction, and bonding, build self-confidence, and encourage teachers to leave their role of knowing what students don't and share the common experience of the trail in the outdoors. I challenge the current notion of overly emphasizing team sports like football when almost every student leaving high school will never play football after graduating, but can learn the same team-building skills from setting up camp, backpacking, and engaging in hiking or related outdoor pursuits—skills they will be able to use *for a lifetime!*

Imagine high school hiking clubs from throughout America, from the Appalachians, the Cascades, the Sierras, the Rockies, etc., all inviting their fellow hikers to join them in their part of the country, during spring breaks, winter recesses, and holidays, for fabulous hiking trips into our wilderness areas—an activity that is free from any element of competition, emphasizing cooperation instead and learning about history (the Old West, early pioneers, American Indians, etc.), geology, or topography, while each student gets to really know another human being, perhaps building friendships that will last a lifetime. If clubs and schools choose to travel to places other than nearby, then the skills of planning, evaluation, team-building, and delegation will also be learned.

Europe has a proud tradition of sports clubs where young people journey to all corners of Europe to bike, ski, play soccer, etc. In Germany, teachers often take a class of fifteen to twenty on a dayhike, where all enjoy the total benefits that hiking offers. It's time for America to rethink its priorities, change social institutions that fail us and values that divide us rather than build community. We still think that building community means helping some needy person, when it can also mean people coming together to "enjoy a common recreational activity freed from competition and pretense."

Colleges can sponsor hiking clubs and outdoor recreation groups, just as they currently sponsor ski clubs. Hiking should be a valid and recognized physical education offering. Professors dayhiking with their students would go a long way in improving faculty-student relationships and support the notion that generations are not separate, but capable of exchanging knowledge, skills, and support whenever possible.

Outdoor Organizations

Hiking clubs, conservation groups, and protectionist agencies like the Sierra Club are perfectly positioned to educate the public as to hiking, trail needs, conservation, and many other related topics. These groups could expand their focus to include more on teaching hiking and outdoor skills and offering hiking trips to the public, along with devoting their energy to protectionist policies—if people are hiking to these wilderness areas, they will vote and act to protect them.

Also, people who have rarely or never hiked, even those in their teens and twenties, because of absent or disinterested parents, want to learn these skills and want to discover the outdoors, if only someone will lead the way. In the 1995 State of the Outdoor Industry Report (published by the Outdoor Recreation Coalition of America and SGMA), it was noted that "the most significant determinant in participation is whether or not one participated in outdoor recreation with his or her family as a child." Outreach to youth groups, co-sponsoring trips with the YMCA/YWCA—all are possibilities that have yet to reach full potential.

Scouting has long been an avenue where youth learned of the outdoors. But my experience with young people has taught me that the older they get, the more they want specific skills or activities. Clubs devoted to just hiking, backpacking, and the like would probably enjoy more interest than anyone now could anticipate.

Government Agencies

State park systems, Bureau of Land Management, U.S. Forest Service, and National Park Service personnel should be freed up and supported in their efforts at educational outreach efforts and hike leading. Career-day activities at schools need to be expanded to adequately represent careers in outdoor recreation, land management, and park services, etc.

Travel Industry

Travel agencies rarely address the topic of outdoor recreational vacations such as noted in chapter 10, The Dayhiking Vacation. Participation in the outdoors could be enhanced if the travel industry helped educate the public as to what outdoor vacation packages are available, having brochures in-office on guided hikes, canoe outfitters, and llama trekking, etc.

Along with this emphasis from the travel industry, hotels that are located in or near outdoor recreational areas could add hiking guide services and trail information as a part of their resources for guests. One of Marriott's flagship hotels offers hiking packages to guests through their Health Spa. As a guide for this hotel, I was very pleased to see wide and enthusiastic interest in this service. Many vacationers want not only something different, but also an exposure to the local landscape coupled with the chance to exercise. Hiking is this perfect activity that satisfies these needs.

Recreational specialists will testify that outdoor adventure vacations are the fastest-growing segment of the vacation industry, and for good reason. Americans recognize that a true vacation should include the opportunity to re-create, rejuvenate, and even learn something in the process. Most people need a stimulating challenge or change of pace from where they came from.

On one New Year's Day I led a group of twenty auto executives on an 8-mile hike through scenic and wild Indian Canyons near Palm Springs, California. None of them missed sitting in front of the television watching football games. It's time that the leisure industry fully recognize and cultivate this growing positive trend in outdoor recreation.

Religious Organizations

As indicated in chapter 9, The Spirituality of Hiking, churches and religious or spiritual groups might increase and even popularize holding services in nature, or conducting retreats and seminars in a natural setting. Deserts, canyonlands, forests, and mountains all offer energizing and inspirational places to be touched by the sacred in nature, giving us needed quiet time to listen for the truths found both within ourselves and in the surrounding natural world. If trails and nature are to be not only used but preserved and enhanced, it will take the powers of both organized and unorganized religion to emphasize the spiritual benefits nature holds for all humankind.

The Private Sector

Corporate America also is forever searching for ways that benefit employees, offer team-building skills, improve communication, and reduce stress in the workplace. Hiking does all of these. People walking together more easily share ideas and discover common ground that supports better cooperation at work. Stress is reduced, as documented in chapter 4, Stress Management and Hiking, and added energy from hiking translates into more productivity in the workplace.

Creativity and enhanced ability to think problems through is also a natural outcome from hiking. Microsoft Corp. encourages supervisors to manage workers' "think time," and offer them opportunities to slow down and get away from the office. Jodi Hobbs, a Microsoft marketing specialist in Phoenix, Arizona, tells that "people at our company know it's part of their job to take an afternoon off to think a problem through. We encourage them to step back and relax and think . . . it's part of our culture, and it keeps us creative." Hobbs' favorite outlet to revitalize is hiking nearby Camelback Mountain. She claims this gives her new perspective.

While traveling near the outskirts of Stockholm in Sweden, I remarked to my host what an impressive-looking university the buildings we were passing represented. He replied that what I was looking at was instead a factory, and that the athletic fields I saw were used each afternoon by all the employees, including the CEO, to play soccer. I thought then, and even more so now, that outdoor recreation together would be an excellent benefit to all involved. Perhaps those work locations where it is feasible to allow an hour or two each week for individual or group hikes ought now be encouraged. We often forget that creative productivity is a function not of time spent hour after hour in one place, but of the energy, motivation, and freedom of the worker while they are at that place.

Hiking as a creative team-builder is also applicable to other organizational needs. Whenever I see politicians, bargaining groups, school boards, etc., bickering, I think to myself that those people badly need to hike together, clear the air, and get a whole new perspective on what's going on. They need to see each other as fellow travelers on the road of life, just as on the trail, instead of a proponent of some differing point of view. Those parents that hike with an individual child in order to build a close but open bond achieve that goal and much more. Adults could gain from following their example.

CARE FOR THE EARTH

Hiking gives many benefits to participants, but it also supports the hiker's taking a new perspective toward the earth and its resources. For years people have politicized the arguments about diminishing natural resources, wilderness, and open spaces. Too often the combatants on both sides argue from an ideological position. How many people fighting over or against open space set-asides have ever walked and hiked through the very places they are fighting about?

We care for those things we value, and we value those things we have direct experience with, experience that fulfills some cherished need of ours. How beneficial it would be for the players in these ongoing debates to hold them at the very sites they are discussing. John Muir had the good fortune in 1903 to actually spend three days in the Yosemite wilderness with President Theodore Roosevelt. The result was that Roosevelt's direct experience with Yosemite encouraged him to become a staunch supporter both of the creation and preservation of not only national parks, but wilderness in general.

The President's Commission on Americans Outdoors in 1988 noted then that "Decisions made between now and the year 2000 will determine the fate of America's remaining land and water resources." Being able to enjoy nature and, more importantly, having a natural world there to enjoy is really the contest between capitalism, business, and media's power to condition all of us with their values and perspective and world view, and the ability of nature's spiritual sanctuary to offer all of us glimpses into other realities than materialism.

The urban environment is a push of commercialism and consumption; nature's environs emphasizes serenity, unconditionality, perspectives into the human heart, beauty, and inner healing. If we lose this resource, what will replace it? If we lose those "special places" where one can still see the horizon with clouds, a tree line, wildflowers, or hear a quiet brook, where else can we go for these spiritual nourishments? The energy and feel of brick, steel, concrete, and plastic is cold, silent, uninviting. Do we want to create a world where the creator is not even welcomed?

Of the many organizations devoted to conservation, The Nature Conservancy (703-841-4850), with over 800,000 members, has helped protect over 8.3 million acres on 1,650 preserves. This dynamic, responsible, and visionary organization seeks to "purchase the deserts, marshes, mountainsides, prairies, islands, and wetlands that are the threatened homes of our planet's rare and endangered plants, animals, and natural communities—to the mutual benefit of all living things." They achieve these goals by "purchasing land, receiving donations of land or conservation easements, forming partnerships with public agencies and private groups, and entering into voluntary agreements with landowners." Many Conservancy preserves are available to hikers, bird-watchers, photographers, and students. Besides protection, their scientists "work to maintain the critical ecological processes of the area." Volunteer opportunities are available, along with a growing community outreach and public education effort. They have consistently demonstrated outstanding leadership on issues important and dear to outdoor enthusiasts worldwide.

The Sierra Club (415-977-5500) is also a national organization (one of the very first such organizations, founded over a century ago by the naturalist John Muir) dedicated to saving America's wildlands. The Sierra Club helps "create and enlarge national parks, designate wilderness areas, preserve forests, prevent destruction of priceless habitats, counter deforestation" and offers club trips and outings to "some of the most spectacular natural areas in the world, from Maine to Madagascar, Patagonia to the Pacific Northwest." This dynamic organization has chapters throughout America.

Perhaps one of the most successful and forward-looking land-use agencies in America is the City of Boulder Open Space Department (303-441-3440). This dynamic Colorado city has preserved over 25,000 acres of surrounding lands as open space. As guided by Boulder's City Charter, the agency directs that Open Space land be acquired, maintained, preserved, retained and used for these purposes: preserving water resources in their natural or traditional state, scenic areas or vistas, wildlife habitats, or fragile ecosystems; preserving land for passive recreation use, such as hiking, photography, nature study, and if specifically designated, bicycling, horseback riding, or fishing; preserving agricultural uses and land suitable for agricultural production; using land for shaping the development of the city, limiting urban sprawl, and disciplining growth; using nonurban land for spatial definition of urban areas; using land to prevent encroachment on floodplains; and preserving land for its aesthetic or passive recreational value and its contribution to the quality of life of the community.

Boulder Open Spaces has developed trail systems to cross open space with the total needs of the user in mind. Some trails allow hikers to visit farmland, riverways, wetlands and animal habitats, geological formations, expansive scenic vistas, historical sites—a virtual "museum walk" out in the open, exposing the user to the complementary benefits of experiencing natural and local history, exercise, aesthetic settings, open space vistas, and freedom from congested city noise and population densities. If every viable urban area in the country followed Boulder's example, trails could be built between urban open space areas, greenbelt corridors that would unite the country along lines of wise land preservation and use. Humanity's return to nature would be complete.

Years ago I began a hiking club that grew quickly. Inquiries about the club so often had to do with what it "cost" to go on a hike with the club. People were taken back to find that there was no cost to hike, just show up with the proper attitude and gear. They were so conditioned to believe that only those things that could be bought with an exchange of currency had value.

Nature cannot be bought; hiking is basically an activity incurring little or no cost. But the cost to all of us if we lose our precious national heritage of "America the beautiful, from sea to shining sea," if there are no longer forests free from the ax and blade and their noise, if the silent deserts become filled in with housing projects, if mountainsides slope down not with fir, pine, aspen, or spruce but with rows of human dwellings, if there are no longer open vistas of many miles without hint of humankind, if the windswept plateaus and mesas become lost in massive developments—then those creative urgings that like a flood burst upon our ancestors when they began trekking those wild landscapes of ages past during the dawn of humankind, urgings that eventually gave rise to religion, philosophy, art, and all of humanity's noble inner spirit—those urgings will subside like the ebb of a tide, whose leaving may very well take our human spirit, our spiritual quest for the promise of the stars and of gentle, kind love and our freedom—with it.

EPILOGUE

Nature is one of the most vital aspects of our living on this planet. It constitutes the physical link between our spirit and heart and our connection with our creator. Hiking is one of the chief ways that we visit these healing and inspirational places—serene lakes, stately mountains, expansive prairies and deserts, seacoasts and wetlands, the healing forests.

Hiking, simplicity itself, takes us away from stress and conflict, offering us sanctuary, time-out, perspective, energizing exercise, a chance to connect to our fellow travelers, creative inspiration and healing, solitude and beauty—and the setting in which we can travel the journey inward and connect with our deepest and true self. Hiking leads us into hallowed places, the cathedral of the forest and mountains, the altar of the mesas and plateaus. We are led but it is we who must accept that invitation and gain all the many benefits that hiking offers her practitioners.

For all the benefits discussed in this book—hike. Let us share our enthusiasm with others. Take another generation with us into the woods and over the cool green hills of Earth, and up into high places and down into vast deserts. Visit the forests, touch the trees, smell them and the wildflowers that scatter about the meadows and along the footpaths. Hike—and find strength to conquer some of life's great challenges, insights to guide our life and peace in the face of mysteries we understand not. Hike—and feel at home again, both on the planet and within ourselves. Hike—and see, finally, that our aloneness, enveloped by the solitude of nature, is a blessing, not a cause for fear. For out of that solitude comes the experience of our wholeness and our oneness with all who share the Earth with us—and the joy of the created in the loving presence of the Creator!

APPENDIX A:
A SAMPLER OF HIKING CLUBS

The following represents some of the hiking clubs located around the United States. For a more complete listing, contact the American Hiking Society, listed in appendix C, Addresses.

Adirondack Mountain Club
814 Goggins Road
Lake George, NY 12845

Adventures for Women
P.O. Box 515
Montvale, NJ 07645

Appalachian Trail Club of Alabama
P.O. Box 381842
Birmingham, AL 35238

Bay Area Ridge Trail Council
311 California Street, Suite 510
San Francisco, CA 94104

Cleveland Hiking Club
P.O. Box 347097
Cleveland, OH 44134

The Coachella Valley Hiking Club
P.O. Box 10750
Palm Desert, CA 92255

Colorado Mountain Club
710 Tenth Street
Golden, CO 80401

Continental Divide Trail Society
3704 North Charles Street, Suite 601
Baltimore, MD 21218

Desert Trail Association
P.O. Box 34
Madras, OR 97741

Finger Lakes Trail Conference
202 Colebourne Road
Rochester, NY 14609

Great Plains Trails Network
3340 South 29th Street
Lincoln, NE 68502

Hawaiian Trail and Mountain Club
P.O. Box 2238
Honolulu, HI 96804

Huachuca Hiking Club
P.O. Box 3555
Sierra Vista, AZ 85636

Ice Age Park and Trail Foundation
P.O. Box 423
Pewaukee, WI 53072

Lone Star Hiking Trail Club
12515 Westmere Drive
Houston, TX 77077

The Mountaineers
1001 SW Klickitat Way, Suite 201
Seattle, WA 98134

Mount Rogers Appalachian Trail Club
153 Kingsbridge
Bristol, TN 37620

Natural Bridge Appalachian Trail Club
P.O. Box 3012
Lynchburg, VA 24503

North Country Trail Association
3777 Sparks Drive SE, Suite 105
Grand Rapids, MI 49546

Northern Plains Region Sierra Club
23 North Scott
Sheridan, WY 82801

Ozark Highlands Trail Association
411 Patricia Lane
Fayetteville, AR 72703

Pacific Crest Trail Association
5325 Elkhorn Boulevard, Suite 256
Sacramento, CA 95842

Pacific Northwest Trail Association
1361 Avon Allen Road
Mount Vernon, WA 98273

Red Lodge Hiking Club
Route 2, Box 3465
Red Lodge, MT 59068

Susquehanna Appalachian Trail Club
P.O. Box 61001
Harrisburg, PA 17106

Tahoe Rim Trail
P.O. Box 4647
Stateline, NV 89449

Taku Conservation Society
1700 Branta Road
Juneau, AK 99801

Washington Trails Association
1305 Fourth Avenue, Suite 512
Seattle, WA 98101

West Virginia Rails-to-Trails Council
P.O. Box 85
Nitro, WV 25143

APPENDIX B:
SOME HIKING DESTINATIONS IN THE UNITED STATES

The following areas of the United States are listed here, to indicate the vast possibilities that exist for hiking vacations. The recreational hiking outlined in key states by no means encompasses all the trails or areas found in those states; instead, these trails and areas are meant as a starting point for you to discover the many opportunities that do exist. The list for California is more extensive than for other states in order to illustrate what kinds of hiking destinations exist in a given state.

THE WEST
California

National Parks: Redwood, Lassen, Yosemite, Kings Canyon, Sequoia, Death Valley, Joshua Tree

Desert Hiking: Palm Springs/Coachella Valley, Anza Borrego Desert State Park, East Mojave National Scenic Area

National Trails: Pacific Crest Trail, American Discovery Trail

Regional Trails: John Muir Trail, Bay Area Ridge Trail

Wilderness Areas: Mount Shasta, Castle Crags, Trinity Alps, Desolation, Carson-Iceberg, John Muir, Golden Trout, San Jacinto, Santa Rosa, Ansel Adams

National Forests: Cleveland, San Bernardino, Angeles, Los Padres, Tahoe, Sequoia, Stanislaus, Shasta-Trinity

State Parks: Big Sur, Cuyamaca, Mount San Jacinto, Big Basin Redwoods

Oregon

National Parks: Crater Lake

National Trails: Pacific Crest Trail, Oregon National Historic Trail

Wilderness Areas: Mount Hood, Cascade Range at Bend, Steens Mountain, Wallowa Mountains, Hells Canyon National Recreation Area, Mount Jefferson, Three Sisters

National Forests: Mount Hood, Willamette, Deschutes

Washington

National Parks: Olympic, Mount Rainier, North Cascades

National Trails: Pacific Crest Trail, Lewis and Clark Trail, Pacific Northwest Trail

Wilderness Areas: Alpine Lakes, Glacier Peak, Mount St. Helens National Volcanic Monument, Mount Baker National Recreation Area, Boulder River Wilderness, William O. Douglas Wilderness, Trapper Creek Wilderness

National Forests: Mount Baker-Snoqualmie, Gifford Pinchot, Olympic

Idaho

National Monuments: Craters of the Moon, Hagerman Fossil Beds

National Trails: California National Historic Trail, Continental Divide National Scenic Trail, Oregon Natural

History Trail, Lewis and Clark National Historic Trail, Nez Perce National Historic Trail

Wilderness Areas: Sawtooth, Gospel Hump

National Forests: Kamiksu, Coeur d'Alene, St. Joe, Clearwater, Nez Perce, Salmon, Payette, Boise, Challis, Targhee, Caribou Cache

Montana

National Park: Glacier

National Trails: Nez Perce Trail, Lewis and Clark National Historic Trail, Pacific Northwest Trail

Wilderness Areas: Bighorn Canyon National Recreation Area, Rocky Mountains, Bob Marshall Wilderness

National Forest: Flathead

Colorado

National Parks: Rocky Mountain, Mesa Verde

Regional Trail: The Colorado Trail

Wilderness Areas: Colorado National Monument, Indian Peaks Wilderness, Boulder Mountain Parks, Flat Tops Wilderness, Collegiate Peaks Wilderness, Holy Cross Wilderness, San Juan Mountains, Maroon Bells-Snowmass Wilderness, Never Summer Wilderness, Lizard Head Wilderness, Uncompahgre Plateau, Black Canyon of the Gunnison

National Forest: Pike and San Isabel

Utah

National Parks: Zion, Bryce Canyon, Capitol Reef, Canyonlands, Arches

Wilderness Areas: Dinosaur National Monument, Flaming Gorge National Recreation Area, High Uintas Wilderness Area, Henry Mountains, Burr Trail, Aquarius Plateau, Pine Valley Mountain Wilderness Area, La Sal Mountains

National Forests: Dixie, Wasatch, Fishlake

New Mexico

National Parks: Carlsbad Caverns, Bandolier National Monument, Gila Cliff Dwellings, White Sands National Monument, Pecos National Monument, Kiowa National Grasslands

National Trails: Santa Fe Trail, Continental Divide Trail

National Forests: Santa Fe, Carson, Cibols, Apache, Gila, Lincoln

Arizona

National Park: Grand Canyon, Petrified Forest National Monument, Canyon de Chelly National Monument, Chiricahua, Sunset Crater, Walnut Canyon National Monument

Regional Trail: The Arizona Trail

Wilderness Areas: Kaibab Plateau, Superstition Mountains, Chiricahua Mountains, Mogollon Rim, White Mountains, Santa Catalina Mountains, Santa Rita Mountains

National Forests: Kaibab, Tonto, Prescott, Coronado, Gila

MIDWEST

Michigan: Isle Royale National Park, North Shore Trail

Missouri: Ozark Trail, The Ozark Forest

Wisconsin: Ice Age National Scenic Trail, North Country National Scenic Trail, Buffalo River Trail, La Crosse River Trail

EAST

New York: Catskill Mountains, Adirondack Park

Pennsylvania: Black Forest-Pine Creek Gorge, Appalachian Trail

Virginia: Shenandoah National Park, Appalachian Trail

NEW ENGLAND

Maine: Baxter State Park, Arcadia National Park, Appalachian Trail

New Hampshire: The Appalachian Trail, The White Mountains

Vermont: The Appalachian Trail, The Green Mountains

APPENDIX C:
ADDRESSES

HIKING AND CONSERVATION ORGANIZATIONS

American Hiking Society
P.O. Box 20160
Washington, DC 20041-2160
(301) 565-6704

American Volkssport Association
1001 Pat Booker Road, Suite 101
Universal City, Texas 78148
(800) 830-WALK

The Nature Conservancy
1815 North Lynn Street
Arlington, VA 22209
(703) 841-5300

The Sierra Club
85 Second St., Second Floor
San Francisco, CA 94105-3441
(415) 977-5500

Guided Hiking Outfitters

Adventure Vacations
7975 East Harvard, Suite J
Denver, CO 80231
(800) 417-2453

America Outdoors (canoeing)
P.O. Box 1348
Knoxville, TN 37901
(202) 543-6870

Backroads (bicycling and hiking)
1516 Fifth Street, Suite Q333
Berkeley, CA 94710-1740
(800) 245-3874

Canadian Mountain Holidays (heli-hiking)
(800) 661-0252

Clearwater Canoe Outfitters
(800) 527-0554

Country Walkers
P.O. Box 180
Waterbury, VT 05676-0180
(800) 464-9255

Earth Treks
RR 2, Box 785
Montville, ME 04941
(800) 589-4770

International Llama Association (llama trekking)
2755 South Locust Street, Suite 114
Denver, CO 80222
(303) 756-9004

New England Hiking Holidays
(800) 869-0949

The Wayfarers
172 Bellevue Avenue
Newport, RI 02840
(800) 849-5087

NATIONAL PARK SERVICE

Headquarters
Department of the Interior
1849 C Street NW, Room 1013
Washington, DC 20240

Alaska Region
2525 Gambell Street
Anchorage, AK 99503

Pacific Northwest Region
83 South King Street, Suite 212
Seattle, WA 98104

Western Region
450 Golden Gate Avenue
Box 36063
San Francisco, CA 94102

Rocky Mountain Region
12795 West Alameda Parkway
P.O. Box 25287
Denver, CO 80225

Southwest Region
P.O. Box 728
Santa Fe, NM 87504

Midwest Region
1709 Jackson Street
Omaha, NE 68102

Southeast Region
Richard B. Russell Federal Building
75 Spring Street SW
Atlanta, GA 30303

Mid-Atlantic Region
143 South Third Street
Philadelphia, PA 19106

National Capital Region
1100 Ohio Drive SW
Washington, DC 20242

North Atlantic Region
15 State Street
Boston, MA 02109

U.S. FOREST SERVICE

Headquarters
The Department of Agriculture
14th Street and Independence Avenue SW
Washington, DC 20250

BUREAU OF LAND MANAGEMENT (BLM)

BLM National Office
Department of the Interior
1849 C Street NW, MS 1000 LS
Washington, DC 20240-0001
(202) 452-7780

BLM Alaska State Office
222 West Seventh Avenue, Suite 13
Anchorage, AK 99513-7599
(907) 271-5555

BLM Arizona State Office
3707 North Seventh Street
P.O. Box 16563
Phoenix, AZ 85011
(602) 640-5547

BLM California State Office
Federal Building 2800, Cottage Way E-2841
Sacramento, CA 95825
(916) 978-4754

BLM Colorado State Office
2850 Youngfield Street
Lakewood, CO 80215
(303) 239-3600

BLM Idaho State Office
3380 American Terrace
Boise, ID 83706
(208) 384-3000

BLM Montana State Office
222 North 32nd Street
P.O. Box 36800
Billings, MT 59107
(406) 255-2808

BLM Nevada State Office
850 Harvard Way
P.O. Box 12000
Reno, NV 89520
(702) 785-6586

BLM New Mexico State Office
1474 Rodeo Road
P.O. Box 27115
Santa Fe, NM 87502-7115
(505) 438-7400

BLM Oregon/Washington
1300 Northeast 44th Avenue
P.O. Box 2965
Portland, OR 97208
(503) 280-7001

BLM Utah State Office
324 South State Street, Suite 301
Coordinated Financial Services Building
Salt Lake City, UT 84111
(801) 524-3146

BLM Wyoming State Office
2515 Warren Avenue
P.O. Box 1828
Cheyenne, WY
(307) 755-6256

BLM Eastern States Office
7450 Boston Boulevard
Springfield, VA 22153
(703) 440-1600

SELECTED STATE PARKS

Arizona State Parks
800 West Washington, Suite 415
Phoenix, AZ 85007
(602) 255-4174

California State Parks
1416 Ninth Street
P.O. Box 942896
Sacramento, CA 94296-0001
(916) 445-2358

Colorado State Parks
1313 Sherman Street, Room 618
Denver, CO 80203
(303) 866-3437

Florida State Parks
Majory Stoneman Douglas Building
Tallahassee, FL 32399
(904) 488-6131)

Georgia State Parks
205 Butler Street
Atlanta, GA 30334
(404) 656-3530

Hawaii State Parks
P.O. Box 621
Honolulu, HI 96809
(808) 548-7455

Illinois State Parks
524 South Second Street
Springfield, IL 62701-1787
(217) 782-6302

Indiana State Parks
608 State Office Building
Indianapolis, IN 46204
(317) 232-4070

Maryland State Parks
Tawes State Office Building
Annapolis, MD 21401
(301) 974-3776

Massachusetts State Parks
100 Cambridge Street
Boston, MA 02202
(617) 727-3180

Michigan State Parks
P.O. Box 30028
Lansing, MI 48909
(517) 373-1207

Minnesota State Parks
500 Lafayette Road
St. Paul, MN 55155-4001
(612) 296-2270

Mississippi State Parks
P.O. Box 23093
Jackson, MS 39225
(601) 961-5300

Missouri State Parks
P.O. Box 176
Jefferson City, MO 65102
(314) 751-2479

New York State Parks
50 Wolf Road
Albany, NY 12233
(518) 457-2475

North Carolina State Parks
P.O. Box 27687
Raleigh, NC 27611
(919) 733-4181

Ohio State Parks
Fountain Square
Columbus, OH 43224
(614) 265-0688

Pennsylvania State Parks
P.O. Box 2063
Harrisburg, PA 17120
(717) 787-6640

Texas State Parks
4200 Smith School Road
Austin, TX 78744
(512) 389-4866

Utah State Parks
1636 West North Temple
Salt Lake City, UT 84116-3156

Virginia State Parks
203 Governor Street, Suite 306
Richmond, VA 23219
(804) 786-2132

Washington State Parks
7150 Cleanwater Lane
Olympia, WA 98504-5711
(206) 753-5757

Author Biographies

Philip Ferranti has hiked the western United States for over twenty years. He has spent much of that time exploring the trails in and near the Palm Springs/Coachella Valley, California, area. During the summer, Philip hikes out of Boulder, Colorado, with the Colorado Mountain Club. Inspired by their organization, he founded the Coachella Valley Hiking Club in 1992, and has guided it to become the fastest-growing hiking club in the United States.

Philip has written for *Backpacker* magazine and contributes hiking columns for local newspapers. In September 1995, he released his first hiking guidebook, *Seventy-Five Great Hikes in and Near Palm Springs and the Coachella Valley*, published by Kendall/Hunt and recognized as a regional best-seller. In April 1996, The Mountaineers published his second outdoor guidebook, *Colorado State Parks: A Complete Recreation Guide*.

As president of Transformation Seminars since 1981, Philip specializes in stress management seminars and "hiking for health and wellness" seminars. He believes that hiking is "one of the most enjoyable and effective stress management programs." Philip is available for consulting, stress management seminars, guided hiking vacations and spa events, and retreats for corporations, organizations, and groups.

Cecilia Leyva is a lifestyle editor for *Profit Publications* magazine in Palm Springs, California. She writes lifestyle features on health, travel, and hiking. As an award-winning journalist, she has covered city government, state and local elections, and human interest stories for local newspapers. In February 1995, she won the Gannett Newspaper Publishing Company's Well-Done Award.

When not writing, Cecilia loves to hike the trails in the Santa Rosa and nearby San Jacinto Mountains. During the summer when the temperatures on the desert floor climb into the triple digits, she heads into higher elevations and cooler weather in Idyllwild. A member of the Coachella Valley Hiking Club since 1992, she hikes regularly on weekends and days off. Last year she spent the summer hiking in the Amazon rain forest and scaled the ancient Incan city of Macchu Picchu, Peru.

AN INVITATION TO OUR READERS

We would welcome your sharing with us your own stories, anecdotes, experiences and motivations – how hiking has positively impacted your life, met your needs, and contributed to your quality of life. This may have happened through the physical/health benefits aspect of hiking, the meeting of new friends, the bonding and communication with significant others, stress management from hiking, creative inspirations, etc. We would love to share what you send us with a larger audience for the purpose of encouraging others to take up this most healthy pastime!

Send your letters to:

Philip Ferranti
42-720 Virginia Avenue
Palm Desert, CA 92211

NOTES

NOTES

NOTES

NOTES

NOTES

NOTES

NOTES

NOTES